UNDAUNTED

MY LIFE AS POLICEMAN AND PRIVATE EYE

JIM SMITH

BLUE LAMP
BOOKS

Revised edition published by Blue Lamp Books 2019
First published by 'Round Midnight Editions (2009, 2013)

ISBN: 978-1-911273-82-0 (paperback)
ISBN: 978-1-911273-75-2 (ebook)

Published by Blue Lamp Books

An Imprint of

Mango Books
18 Soho Square
London
W1D 3QL

www.MangoBooks.co.uk

UNDAUNTED

To HELEN

[handwritten inscription]

Dedicated to my wife, Janet,
who stood by me through the good and bad times.
Without her help, I could not have survived the bad times.

UNDAUNTED

FOREWORD

We all meet one or more individuals who make a lasting impression on us. Jim Smith is one of these individuals. I was an Inspector with eighteen years' service when I took charge of 3 Unit Special Patrol Group, which consisted of thirty-four officers. Jim was already in 3 Unit; he was a natural 'plainclothes man'. Not the largest of men, his appearance fooled many a villain and he had an outstanding record for apprehending serious criminals. Moreover, as a keen photographer, he would spend many hours off-duty in central London using his uncanny knack of spotting 'dodgy characters'. Jim would then process the pictures and send them to various departments throughout the police. I would often receive requests from those departments to 'borrow' Jim for one or more days. I should also mention his good sense of humour, which I enjoyed even when it was at my expense.

Jim was selected for the Criminal Intelligence Department (C11) at Scotland Yard and left the unit. I left the unit on promotion and lost contact with him. I was not surprised, however, to learn that he was lecturing the Chief Inspectors course at Bramshill Police College on the work of the Criminal Intelligence Department.

Obviously, I heard of the incident involving the Indian High Commission which led to the shooting of two people in the group who had taken hostages there. Jim was awarded the British Empire Medal for his courage during that incident. It was soon after this that he was transferred out of C11. It was clear to me that Jim's departure occurred under unpleasant circumstances and led to his resignation from the force.

He shortly after became a private investigator, and with his police background and natural ability, he was very successful in the field.

This book may answer the question: Why did he leave the work he enjoyed so much? Up to and including his time with the SPG, Jim had worked with uniformed officers and had had occasional contact with the CID. Throughout my service, I also had many contacts with that branch. I met many who were good policemen with respect for the uniform officers, but there were others whose actions were questionable. Like Jim, I was at times inclined to put my misgivings 'on paper', but my experience was that doing so was unlikely to successfully bring about change.

In this book you will see that Jim Smith feels he was 'targeted' by senior officers seeking to protect their own dishonest activities. Unable to breach the protective barriers of this cabal within the CID, Jim was eventually forced to give up the work he loved.

I treasure my friendship with Jim, and we keep in touch regularly. I know that since leaving the Force he has given major assistance to the police, often where serving officers got the credit for the success. He has also given valuable assistance to others who were being victimised.

This book is not a work of fiction. I wish it every success.

Les David
Chief Inspector Metropolitan Police (Retired)

INTRODUCTION

Even though it didn't start out that way, this book is ultimately about change. Change in a country that came out of a war wondering if winning was all it was cracked up to be. Change in a period when the shackles of austerity gave way to new found freedoms with completely different ways of thinking and behaving. Change recorded over two-dozen years, as seen through the eyes of someone who believes in tradition and progress. Change in society, change in policing and change in criminality.

I lived through it both as a policeman and a member of the public, seeing and being intrigued, determined, honoured and bemused by the good, the bad and the ugly in both of these worlds. The innocence and honour of the force of the early 1960s, the corruption of a great institution, my betrayal by a great institution, the rise of the tabloid criminal, the humanity and lack of humanity of so-called hard men, the realities of crime, punishment and exercise of law and order.

I am Jim Smith, and this is my story.

ONE

THE END OF THE BEGINNING, 1974

'Good afternoon, my name is Chief Inspector Batchelor, I believe we met when I was investigating a murder on Tower Bridge's patch.'

'Yes, that's when I was at C11, Criminal Intelligence, New Scotland Yard,' I replied.

'Yes, I thought so.'

I looked at the two CID (Criminal Investigation Department) officers who accompanied him. They sat, expressionless, in the small interview room at Romford Police Station.

'Well, I'm afraid we are here today under much different circumstances. Have you any idea why we are here?'

'No, Sir.'

Of course I did.

'Well, let me tell you. We have come here to interview you with a view to you being charged under the Official Secrets Act, for stealing an official document from C11. Now do you understand?'

OSA? What's he on about? Stealing?

'Well?' he asked.

Charged? I hadn't done a bent thing during my twelve years of Police service. This was a fit-up, not by Batchelor but by someone much higher; Commander Dilley of New Scotland Yard immediately sprang to mind.

'Jock, you've got a good police record, as good as many and

better than most. Bloody hell, you're up for the British Empire Medal, so let's not mess about. You know the score.'

Yes, I knew the score. Why hasn't he cautioned me, if he's got the evidence?

'You see, Jock, you are captured bang to rights.'

'Bang to rights, what are you talking about?'

He looked over to the other officers, gesturing to his briefcase. His 'bag carrier'[1] picked it up and put it on the table. Batchelor opened it, removed a copy of the *News of the World*, spread the paper on the table in front of me and nodded at the front page.

'Recognize the picture?'

It was a front-page spread of a picture I had taken of a female who had been blackmailing a 'Mr X'.

I sat in silence looking into the police station yard where PCs were going about their business. It was life as normal as they laughed and joked. Yesterday, I had been doing the same. I lost track of the passing time; it could have been a few seconds, a minute or a quarter of an hour. My head was spinning, my stomach was knotted. I just kept thinking, OSA? What's this all about?

'Well, what have you got to say?'

'I'm thinking.'

'I'd have a good think if I were you, Jock, because at the moment I don't think you are thinking. This is a serious matter; you could end up doing time for this.'

I continued to stare into the station yard. I had never taken anything from C11. What was this all about?

'Jock, look at the picture, have you seen it before?'

'Of course I've seen it before, I took it.'

'That's better, now we are getting somewhere. We know you took it, we know when, how and why. We even know you took a bird from the *News of the World* into the C11 office and showed

1 A detective sergeant so nicknamed from the time when the Met did all murder enquiries throughout the country. The bag contained exhibit labels, fingerprinting kit and other accoutrements for such an enquiry and was carried by a junior officer on behalf of his boss. The name has stuck ever since.

her the indices. It's 'hands up' time, Jock. A quick statement from you and then we can all go home, eh, what about it?'

Home? More likely down into the cells for me and then they can all go home. Why were they treating me like an idiot?

A quick statement and then we can all go home! I must have used the expression hundreds of times when I was dealing with criminals over the years. Anyway, who's the bird from the *News of the World*? He's flannelling.

'So, what about it?' he asked, looking me in the eye.

'When I said I took it before, I mean I was the photographer.'

He reached to his briefcase, took out some statement forms and placed them on the desk.

It shouldn't be like this, this was the job I loved and had given up so much for. If I had stayed in uniform, I would never have been in this mess.

'Yeah, guv, I'll make a statement,' I said.

He looked at his two colleagues, winked and pushed the statement forms towards me. I had nothing against Batchelor. Except one Commander, and that was Dilley, I had never heard anyone else say a bad word about him.

Had I remained in uniform, I would never have worked under some of the most corrupt police officers that Scotland Yard had ever known. These very men were bigger villains than the people they were supposed to be catching. At least the villains knew what they were; in their own way they were honest in that they openly admitted to being criminals. I never heard a cop admit to being bent. In years to come I would hear both serving and retired officers refer to these corrupt officers as 'Old Rascals', almost as a term of endearment.

'Well, you might as well write it, Jock, you've done a few in your time.'

There were hushed sighs of relief in the room. I pushed the statement forms back to him.

'No, guv, you write it please.'

'No problems. Here, you write it for Jock, that's what you get paid for.'

And with that he pushed the statement forms to his sergeant, who took a pen from his pocket, repositioned the forms and stared straight at me.

'OK, full name and date of birth,' the sergeant said.

I stared across the desk as the three of them stared back. All the years of being a good and honest cop were about to go out of the window, and it was a corrupt Commander and his associates who were going to see to it that I was pushed. I gazed down at the top of the desk, the last twelve-plus years rushed through my mind.

I looked up, took a deep breath and started.

'James Smith, Eleven, Six, Forty-one…'

TWO

A GOVAN BOY: THE BEGINNING

Eleven, Six, Forty-one... a midwife hands a baby boy to his mother. His feet are sticking out from under his shawl.

'Here's Jimmy the Bobby!'

That was my introduction into the world, and these words were repeated to me by my mother, Catherine, throughout her life.

My birthplace, Argaty House, the ancestral home of the former Prime Minister Sir Alec Douglas-Home, had been commandeered by the government and transformed into a maternity hospital during the war. Although only some sixty miles from Glasgow, it was a very long way from my parents' tenement flat at 4, Crossloan Place, Govan, Glasgow. Govan's motto: 'Nothing without Labour'. Govan was a drab, grey place, its streets lined with rows of tenements. The back courts where once grass had grown were now hard-packed soil, with clothespoles marking out the area of the former drying greens. All tenements at one time had outside wash houses with large open-topped copper boilers. The boilers had been vandalized and any metal had found its way to scrap metal dealers.

Our house was on the top floor of the two-storey building. The ground floor entrance had a passageway, 'the close', which led into the backyard. Most of the iron railings had been cut down to assist in the war effort, the ones remaining had been bent and twisted to give people a short-cut to adjoining streets. Despite the rundown condition of the back courts, the close and the staircases were mostly kept spotless by the residents, who swept them daily and scrubbed the staircases each Friday afternoon.

On the last flight of stairs to our flat was an ornamental wrought-iron balustrade with a highly-polished mahogany handrail. Hanging from the handrail was a canvas sack which was for discarded paper. Waste food was put in a pig swill bin. These items were collected twice a week; household waste was collected at night by the 'bin men', who wore hats not unlike miners' helmets, complete with lamps. They drove electric dustcarts, which were nicknamed 'the ghost train' due to the lack of any engine noise as it moved. Late-night revellers would sing as they passed the carts, much to the annoyance of the workers, the words were sung to the opening bars of the Colonel Bogey march and went as follows: 'We are the night shite-shifters, we shift shite by night.' This was followed by a loud cheer.

Were these systems put into place to reduce the 'carbon footprint', or encourage 'recycling', phrases unheard of at the time? No, they were done because it made sense.

Our flat consisted of a lobby with a small toilet at one end and a wardrobe and coal bunker at the other. The front room was kept for special occasions and had a 'hole in the wall' - not a cash point, but a recess where a double bed was hidden behind a curtain. The back room too had a 'hole in the wall', and a grate with a built-in oven and a hotplate for cooking. The heating for this was from the fire, which had to be kept alight summer and winter, topped up by coal from the bunker.

The coalman would make his deliveries in sacks carried on his shoulders, his only protection a leather apron which hung over his back and a dirty coal-stained cap which was moulded onto his head by the bags. I could never imagine it had ever been washed. Coal delivery days were hated by my mother. In the winter, the bags would be carried up the stairs soaking wet from the open horse and cart. A trail of black sludge marked out the coalman's delivery route as he climbed his way up the stairs shouting 'coal', sounding like some castrated Alpine yodeller. Mother would walk behind the bag with her hands either side to stop the bag from touching the lobby walls.

Summer was different. It was a case of making sure all internal doors were closed in an attempt to control the cloud of coal dust which emerged as the contents of the bag spilled into the bunker.

During the winter of 1947 Britain had the heaviest snowfall for years. This caused all coal deliveries to be stopped. I still have memories of the three of us, my sister Catherine, my mother and myself, trying to push an old pram to the coal yard at Govan Cross and digging into the snow-drifts to fill bags with any coal we could find. Good fun for us children, but terrible times for my parents, who struggled throughout these hard times with my father going to work as usual through hail, rain or snow. He often arrived home soaked to the skin and my sister and I had to go into the 'good room' and wait until our father had stripped off and washed at the sink.

The sink, which was against the window, had a brass swan-neck tap, polished to perfection and it supplied the only washing and drinking water to the house. The draining board was made of pine, which over the years had been scrubbed white. Baths and showers were taken in the public baths just round the corner. It was a common sight to see families walking to the baths with their towels rolled up under their arms.

It was a tough life, with food and clothing shortages, but we took it as it came as we didn't know of any better.

Nobody in Govan had country views. Our view from the rear window was a storage yard for Harland and Wolff, the shipbuilders. It had loads of places where we played hide and seek, and without doubt we were putting our lives at risk when we crawled in and out of all sorts of metal structures.

Govan people are proud and generally very honest. 'Och aye we wid huv a wee bit of stuff oot of the yard, a bit of wood, a poker for ma Mammy's fire, but nothing big.'

The story goes that one of the workers was cutting a used paint tin in half and growing seedlings in them. When the time came to take them home, he would wrap the tin in a newspaper with the plants sticking out of the top. When the yard horn sounded to end a shift, a tidal wave of workers would flood out of the large sliding gates. Anyone carrying anything would be stopped by the yard 'Polis'.

'Hey you, whit you got there?'

'Jist some plants that av been 'bringin on' in the heat next to the boilers.'

'Gees a gander,' and with that the Polis examined the plants.

'Aye, OK, don't forget tae bring us some tomatoes!'

'Aye, nae bother.'

This continued for a few nights.

'Mair plants Wullie?'

'Aye, they're fair comin' on'

And with that, the Polis waved him through. And so it continued for six days, after which Fairfield's were six gallons of paint light. How? Easy, just put a bit of soil on top of the paint tins with the plants sticking out and then wrapped these tins in a copy of a newspaper. 'Easy Peasey!' I still use a stainless steel shoehorn in the shape of Betty Grable's leg complete with suspenders which was made in Fairfield's yard in 1945.

My father Wallace, a Glasgow policeman, was stationed at Govan Police Station where he served as a War Reserve Officer. Amongst his duties was to guard Prince's Docks, albeit with a pistol with no ammunition.

My first recollection of anything to do with the police was sitting on a desk in a police box at the gates of Prince's Docks. The date was 8th May, 1945 - VE Day. Searchlights from the ships were pointing skywards in 'V' shapes and fireworks soared into the sky. It was some years later that I was to discover the 'fireworks' were tracer shells being fired from the many ships tied up in the docks.

Crossloan Place, long since gone, not destroyed by Jerry's bombs but demolished by Glasgow Corporation, was a small cul-de-sac of grey-stone tenements. No red sandstone here, they were for 'toffs'. In the middle of the street were two brick-built air raid shelters.

On Victory night someone had built a bonfire in the street. The wooden-slatted benches from inside the shelters had been ripped out and 'piled up to the sky' on top of the bonfire. A figure of Hitler was hanging from the 'big lamp-post' in the side of the road. It was electric! The 'wee lamp posts' were gas! Mrs Campbell, a large woman who always seemed to be dressed in black, came running out of her house. 'Cut that thing doon! Cut him doon, that's ma man's biler boiler suit. A' used a load of coupons fir that biler suit.'

The rope round Hitler's neck was soon cut and down he came and was thrown onto the bonfire, complete with Mr Campbell's biler suit. Everyone was cheering and laughing. No more bombs, no more 'men and sons' going to war. Folk were dancing up and down the street. I am told that as I was put to bed by my mother, my sister Catherine told me that the war was over and there would be no more bombs, no more air raid sirens and no more running down the stairs to the air raid shelters. Apparently my reply was, 'Can we now get eggs?'

Some days later, an RAF plane flew over Glasgow leaving a vapour trail in the shape of a 'V' for Victory sign in the sky, no doubt to boost peoples morale - unlike the Luftwaffe aircraft that had flown over Govan less than a month after the outbreak of war and left a swastika vapour trail in the sky. It also photographed the whole of Govan. These pictures were used for a daylight bombing raid on 19th July, 1940. They would be used again later for the bombing raids on the 13th, 14th and 15th of March, 1941, when 250 bombers bombed Glasgow and the surrounding area, killing 647 people and seriously damaging 6,835 houses. The aerial photographs were retrieved from Nazi archives after the war, and clearly show Harland and Wolff's shipyards along with many more targeted industrial sites.

I was brought up in a Salvation Army environment in Govan Citadel. There was a routine that had to be followed. Sunday morning, Sunday school, back for dinner and then back to 'The Hall' for Sunday afternoon Sunday School, and then down the stairs and into an afternoon service. After this, it was back home for tea and back to the Sunday evening meeting. It was a way of life and I never thought too much about it. After all, my grandfather had carried the Salvation Army's 'Blood and Fire' flag in front of the funeral procession of William Booth, the founder of the Salvation Army, who had been laid to rest in Stoke Newington Cemetery in London.

I attended Greenfield School, a 'Prodie' school where discipline and the three Rs were hammered home, not literally with a hammer, but with a three-foot leather belt cut into thongs at one end. It was issued to each teacher by Glasgow Corporation. Some teachers took delight in telling their class, 'I bought my own.'

Opposite our school was St Constantine's, a school where 'the Catholics' went. Prodies were not allowed to go there!

When away from school my playground was in the backcourts of Govan tenements, playing between the air raid shelters and the 'midges'. Basically, the midges were a brick structure about four feet high, the roofs were of reinforced concrete. They could hold about six square dustbins. The midges were used as a jumping station onto the side of the air raid shelters, where we would do a 'clingy' - throwing yourself at the side of the shelter and catching onto the flat roof with outstretched arms and pulling ourselves onto the roof to the cheers of the rest of our gang - all four of us aged between eight and nine years old. It is not until we were much older did we realize just how much danger we were putting ourselves in.

There were many, 'I dare you' games, one that was perhaps the most dangerous of them all. The lamplighters carried a pole to reach up to the gas street lights. On the end of the pole was a key which was used for turning on the coal gas, which was ignited my means of the flame on the end of the pole. This polished-brass end contained a mixture of carbide and water, which in turn produced an inflammable gas to produce the flame on the end of the pole. On the completion of his round the lamplighter would empty the unused mixture into the gutter. This usually dried out by the following morning, leaving a crystallized powder for our 'dare'. The person accepting the dare would spit on the palm of his hand and then deposit the powder on the spittle. To continue the dare, the arm had to be held at right angles to the body as a chemical reaction took place on the palm of the outstretched hand. The rest of the gang would then shout 'One, two, three' as they counted out the time the bubbling, burning mixture was held. If I remember correctly, the highest number reached was five before the blistered hand was thrust into a mucky puddle.

Dangerous games played by children out of sight of their parents, but although we made our own dangers, we lived in a safe area.

I can only once remember being told to stay away from one

person, who was a road sweeper. We didn't ask why, it was sufficient to be told to stay away. I later discovered that the man had exposed himself to children. Police were not involved; the local men administered justice 'up a close'.

We had Catholics in our gang, but that didn't matter as long as we were not at the same school. What a crazy mixed-up situation.

My father left the police and returned to his pre-war job. This didn't stop police visiting our home. The 'beat men' would come up the stairs to our house. My mother would make tea for them while my father would talk 'police stories', and I would sit on the floor listening and taking in every word. Tam Young, one of the local policemen, would sit at the piano and serenade us with tunes ranging from The Old Rugged Cross to Run Rabbit Run. No doubt these meetings had a big influence on my future. One thing is for sure, I can never remember wanting to be anything else other than a policeman.

At the age of ten my family moved to Eastwood, on the outskirts of Glasgow. This was a new development of houses by the Glasgow Corporation for 'nice' families. The houses had all mod cons; bathrooms with hot and cold running water, a kitchen with a cooker, three bedrooms and a garden. This was luxury, and brought a sense of self-respect to the family.

Up until the time my mother met my father, she had lived with her parents in Dalton Villa, a luxury residence in Merryland Street, a short distance from Ibrox Park, the home of Glasgow Rangers Football Club. Her father had made his money through fish and chip shops. She and her six brothers had been brought up in an environment with a housekeeper running the home, and the children attending fee-paying schools. This wealth was to disappear after the death of her mother in childbirth. Pop Morris, as my Grandfather became known, shipped three of his sons - Aaron, James and John - off to Australia through a scheme set up by the Salvation Army's Hadleigh Farm Colony in the 1890s to train people in agricultural skills and give them the opportunity to move from the squalor of London and other large cities. She would not see two of her brothers for another 44 years. The other brother, John, died before he could return home.

Apparently, it was Pop Morris' intention to sell up in Glasgow and with the rest of the family follow the boys to Australia. This plan was short-lived, as when at the age of twelve my mother, on returning from school, was greeted by a woman she had never seen before. Pop Morris' words remained with her until her dying day: 'This is your new Mother.'

Things went downhill from that day, when his new wife moved in with her sons from a previous marriage. The business folded, the new wife opened a drapery shop and made my mother work in it. The villa was sold and the money vanished, and Pop Morris and his new wife moved into rented accommodation.

In his later years he spent a lot of his time collecting driftwood from the River Clyde and pushing it home on a handcart to cut it up for firewood. I was with my mother on one occasion when she saw him struggling along the opposite side of the road with his fully-laden barrow. To me he looked like a rag-and-bone man. She walked over to him as he stood next to the barrow in his old clothes. He barely looked up. I don't know what was said, but they both stood hugging each other as the tears ran down their faces. Were they talking of much happier times, when they were together as a family? I don't know, but perhaps a letter she received sometime later from my Uncle John gave some clues. The letter was received by my mother after she had written to him telling him of his father's death. I only discovered it after my mother's death in 2001. It was dated '5.11.56', and came from Bexley, Sydney. Some of it read:

> Dear Cathie,
>
> It is with a sad heart that I write to you tonight. I never thought I would be so upset over Daddy's death. I am using the word Daddy as that is all we knew him as.
>
> Well Cathie while I am sitting here writing and there are things going through my mind about our family. Cathie, we can all thank God we had a good Father and Mother and they were good Christians, for which I am thankful.
>
> I will never forget the morning when Daddy came upstairs and told us Mother had died. As you know Cathie, I had some hard feelings about our Father, but tonight I can only think about the good things about him. He was a stern man, but a good and godly man. I think I knew more

about him than anyone else [in] the months after mother died. As you know I slept in the same room as him and many a night I woke up to find him on his knees praying to God to help him to be a mother and a father to us, all which I am sure he was, although a very deep man.

The letter gives a little bit of an insight into the way things were. After the death of Pop Morris and his 'new wife', my mother never received as much as a keepsake.

It was not until the age of nineteen when my mother met my father, a drapery traveller, that things changed. They were married two years later and remained married for 57 years, up until the time of my father's death.

I moved to Carnwadric Primary School in Capelrig Street, then after my qualifying exam, the 'Qualy', it was onto Shawlands Academy. Unbeknownst to me I was walking in footsteps of one of the world's most notorious child killers. I had shared the very playground where Ian McLean played. McLean later changed his name to Ian Brady and, together with Myra Hindley, became the infamous 'Moors murderers', the killers of numerous children. They were later jailed for life.

At the age of sixteen it was time to leave school and earn some money. I met the careers officer with my father. To me there seemed very little point in meeting him; in my mind I knew what I wanted to do, and that was to join the police. Before getting into the car my father gave me some advice: 'You can forget anything about the police… you'll get a trade behind you!' I am sure he said this for all the right reasons, but reasons I couldn't see at that time. We drove to the meeting in his Morris Traveller. Not a word was spoken. We eventually arrived at Shawlands Academy and made our way into the interview room.

'Come in, Jim, Mr Smith, sit down.' The careers officer looked me up and down. 'Yes, I have looked at your reports and see that you have done well on technical subjects and art. Let's see what we have for you!'

He then sifted through some papers and looked up. 'Yes, we have a few apprenticeships available, we have one here for a TV mechanic in Cathcart. What do you think of that?' Silence.

'Yes or no, would you like to go for an interview? I can arrange it.'

'No, I don't think so.'

'Well, what would you like to do, you must have some idea?'

My father interrupted and blurted out, 'He's got it into his head that he would like to join the police, but of course, he's too young for that and besides he should get a trade before he does any of that.'

'There is a Cadet's scheme at…' I interrupted.

My father stared at me.

'So, you would like to join the police. Well, as you rightly say there is a Cadet scheme, I think it's at Paisley.'

I interrupted again.

'Yes, it's Paisley, they have a junior Cadet scheme where you can start at sixteen and then at eighteen you can become a senior cadet and then go into the police at nineteen. The pay…'

My father interrupted at that stage.

'Well, you're not tall enough for that so listen to what the man says.'

I sat between them as they exchanged winks and nods. I can't remember much more about the meeting other than I ended up going for an interview for a TV mechanic - the job of the future!

I failed the interview. One up for Jim!

A few days later we received a visit from a neighbour, a Mr Hay.

'I understand your Jim's looking for a job as an apprentice.'

I could only hear parts of the conversation, so I crept down the lobby stairs.

'Aye, Andrew Dixon's at Pollokshaws are looking for a boy, if you like I'll put a word in for him.'

It was a done deal! A week later I was into my overalls, 'Tuff boots' and off to work with my new folding three-foot rule in the rule pocket in my overalls. Five years training as an apprentice joiner and two nights a week in the winter months studying at Stow College.

I hated every minute of that job. I counted off every day in a diary until I had served my time. The most ridiculous thing about it was that I would play truant from night school and read books on Scottish Law.

I continued to play in the Govan Salvation Army band. On one occasion, whilst visiting the house of a Salvationist, he mentioned to me that whilst he had been collecting insurance money a woman had pointed out a yard behind a tenement building in the Anderston district of Glasgow. The woman had said, 'See that big shed in there, there is a lorry full of 'pinched' butter in there. The guys in the yard are selling it dead cheap.'

I got the address and went to the first phone box and in some panic dialled the number of Glasgow Police Headquarters.

'Glasgow Police Headquarters, can I help you?' a woman asked.

'I know where there is a load of butter.'

'Aye, so do I son... doon at the Co-Op,' she started to laugh. 'Who is it you want to speak to?'

'No, this butter's been stolen and it's on a big lorry.'

'Hold on a wee minute.'

I held on.

'Hello, CID, Detective Sergeant Watts speaking, can I help you?'

'I don't want to give my name but if you go up a close at number 7 such and such a street, go to the top floor and look out the stairhead window into the yard behind the back court... You'll see a big shed with a tarpaulin hanging over the end. Inside the shed is a lorry that's been stolen and it's full of butter.'

I didn't stop to take a breath.

'Hey, hang on a wee minute.'

I could hear him talking: 'Wullie, there's a kid here says that that lorry load of butter is in –' I couldn't hear any more.

'Can I have your name son?'

'No, no I don't want to get involved.'

'No, it's just you will get money for it if this is right.'

'No, no that's OK, I'll phone you tomorrow.'

'Whit's your first name?'

'Eh, just call me Billy.'

'OK, Billy, gee's a ring back the morra.'

I put the phone down, I was filled with excitement. I couldn't tell anyone. The next 24 hours dragged - my first job with the police!

Back to the phone box.

'CID, Sergeant McCloud, can I help you?'

'Sergeant Watts, please.'

'Hi - hold on... it's for you... who wants him?'

'Billy.'

'It's Billy.' I could hear in the background the voice of Sergeant Watts.

'Gee's the phone, it's the butter boy. Hello Billy.'

'I phoned you yesterday about the butter.'

'Aye, I know who you are Billy.'

'Aye, okay.'

'That was great what you told me yesterday. We 'lifted' three 'Neds' yesterday mornin' and got the butter and the lorry. Come and see us and we'll get you a reward.'

'No, I canny.'

'Why not?'

'Oh, it's just because... just because. Is it OK if I hear of any other things can I phone you?'

'Dead right you can, but pop in and see us anyway, Billy.'

I hung up. I never told a soul about it.

I continued working on various joinery jobs for Dixon's throughout Glasgow and the surrounding area for a year or so, then while on one job, right out of the blue, a joiner I was working with casually said to another joiner, 'You know these forged tickets for the big game that's coming up, my mate's printing them.'

'Oh, yir arse!'

'No, I'm no kiddin'. He's a printer down at the Co-Op print works at Shieldhall and they're doing them doon there.'

'Can you get me two?'

'Aye nay bother here,' and with that he handed him two tickets. 'Gee's five bob for the two.'

'Done.'

As soon as 4 o'clock came and I was finished at the job, I was on my bike and down the road like a rocket to the nearest phone box.

With trembling hands I inserted a penny and dialled the

THREE
HENDON AND
THE WICKET GATE

Eventually, I did gain enough weight to re-apply for the Metropolitan Police.

The long-awaited letter arrived from the Met telling me I had been accepted for a preliminary interview and exam at Glasgow's Oxford Street Police Station.

I attended the exam room. There were about thirty of us; most were applicants for the City of Glasgow Police. The examination consisted of spelling and general education questions to make sure candidates were not completely thick. As we sat at our desks, a typical big 'Glasgow Polis', a sergeant with a strong Highland accent mixed with a Glasgow slang, stood at the front of the room. 'James Smith?'

I raised my hand.

'Aye, I see you are going to join the wee midgets in the Met Polis.'

I was the smallest in the room, and he wasn't going to let me forget it. 'If that pencil's too big for you, we've got some wee ones for Met recruits oot the back if you canny manage wae the big yins the Glasgow Polis use!'

I answered the questions and the papers were collected by the 'chuchter'.

'Right that's it, you can awe go hame and we'll be in touch.'

I got the impression he couldn't finish the class quick enough to enable him to have a 'wee dram'.

The papers were sent off to the Metropolitan Police, and sometime later I received instructions to attend the Recruitment Centre in Borough High Street in London. I travelled down to London by train, and underwent my assessment: medical, education and oral examinations. Out of 41 candidates at this assessment, only seven passed. I was one of the seven.

We were taken to another room and informed that we had been accepted, subject to the usual inquiries being carried out. One of these was for my home to be examined by Glasgow police to see if it was fit and proper for an officer of the Metropolitan Police.

A few days later a letter arrived telling me that I had been accepted. A few more days passed, after which an inspector and sergeant from Glasgow Police attended my place of employment where they spoke to the foreman. The sergeant was the one from my Glasgow exam. As he crossed the yard he recognized me and walked over. 'Yir gaffer says you'll make a better Polis than a Jiner!'

On Sunday, 27th May, 1962 my family and friends came to Glasgow Central Railway Station and waved me off. I had achieved my life-long ambition and was on my way to join the Police.

The train journey took approximately sixteen hours. The guard walked down the corridor and explained the delay was due to work in progress… nothing changes.

Eventually the train pulled into Euston Station and I made my way to the Police recruitment centre at Borough High Street. A warden booked me in and I was shown to my cubicle, a wooden-sided box with a curtain acting as a door.

On 28th May, 1962, we were loaded into a bus and taken to Peel House Training School. We were sworn in as constables of the Metropolitan Police. We took the Oath of Allegiance to Her Majesty the Queen.

Next, we were fitted with our uniforms. Without fail, everyone walked around in civvies wearing their helmets and carrying numerous pieces of uniform. We were a motley crew made up of a London bus driver, an ex-army officer, a bricklayer, a former Irish Guardsman, and many more occupations. Oh yes, and a former Roman Catholic Priest.

We were each given an Instruction Book - an IB. The policeman's Bible.

We were introduced to the drill sergeant. 'Right you lot, on to the bus and go to your new home - Hendon Police College - for the next thirteen weeks. On the journey, learn the first two pages of your Instruction Book word-perfect. You will be tested on it tomorrow morning.'

We arrived at Hendon College and were shown to our rooms, four to each room.

The drill sergeant, an ex-Guardsman, dressed as if going on parade, crashed the door open and stamped into the room.

'Be in the laundry room in five minutes.'

We mumbled, 'Yes, sir,' 'Yes, Sergeant,' and simply, 'Yes.'

The laundry room had rows of ironing tables and washing machines down one wall. We waited by the tables and the door crashed open yet again. 'Right you lot, first things first! I am a Sergeant, not a Sarge, nor a Sir; do you understand?'

'Yes, Sergeant.'

'You sound like a bunch of fucking Girl Guides. When I ask you a question you will answer, addressing me as "Sergeant" at all times and you will answer loud enough for me to hear you. Do you understand?'

'Yes, Sergeant!' echoed around the room.

This seemed to please him. He bent down and picked up a pair of boots from the floor. 'Are these boots clean?'

They looked clean to us. Three or four of us answered. 'Yes, Sergeant!'

'Bollocks, they are not clean enough for the Metropolitan Police!'

He glared at us. 'These are clean.' He pointed to his own boots. He took two paces forward and brought his foot down with a thundering crash. Our reflections could be seen in the toecaps.

'That's the standard you will bring yours to. I want them like that by tomorrow morning when you parade. Do you understand?'

'Yes, Sergeant!'

'Do you have any questions?'

Silence. Then a voice from the back of the laundry room spoke out.

'How do we get them like that Sergeant?'

'Where's the fucker with the squeaky voice that asked that?'

'It was me, Sergeant, I was wondering how…' The former priest never got another word out.

'Are you a poof?'

The recruit looked in amazement. 'No, Sergeant,' he replied.

'Well, you sound like one. Ask me again.'

'How do we get our boots like yours?'

'I'm sure you're a poof. What did you do before you joined this lot?'

'I was in the brotherhood, Sergeant.'

'What, the fucking Masons?'

'No, Sergeant, the Roman Catholic brotherhood. I was a priest.'

'Well, how do you know you're not a poof if you've not even tried any of it? Did you try it and not like it?'

Silence.

'Now, in answer to your question, you will use Kiwi polish, water and a yellow duster.'

Silence.

'OK, let's show you how to press your uniform for Mister Wall in the morning.'

Little did I realize how hard the next thirteen weeks would be. In fact, two members of the class couldn't keep up with the pace. They packed their bags and during the night left the training college. The following morning we found their beds empty. Their uniforms neatly folded and a note on top of each, which read: RESIGNED.

The College Commandant was Superintendent Tommy Wall, a large man about six feet tall who weighed near twenty stone. He was noted for his bullying and swearing at constables on parade. Woe betide any officer who came on parade with as much as a speck of dust on their uniform; Tommy Wall would 'have them'.

His favourite trick was to appear midway through the morning parade, saunter across the parade square and walk up to an unsuspecting recruit and stare at him or her.

'Are those semen stains on the Commissioner's trousers?'

us they can get out walk over and then we talk.'

'Hoy, John,' a cry from the driver.

'Ignore him,' Yogi said.

'John, hoy, Aldgate East?' Another plea. Beep, beep, the car horn sounded again. 'Where's Aldgate East?'

'Come on, let's have a word with this Tosser,' Yogi said.

I walked with my 'trainer' to the car, he looked down at the driver. 'Don't sound your warning instrument when you are stationary. It's an offence, OK?'

'Warning instrument, what's that then, John?' the driver asked.

'Your horn. That's the first thing. Secondly, how did you know my name was John?'

'I just guessed, didn't I?'

'Well, guess your bleeding way to Aldgate East.' With that he walked off, swiftly followed by me, my new-found 'colleague' mumbling to himself, 'Tosser, I hate bleeding tossers!'

Yogi had an 'answer' for any question put to him. We were on parade on early-turn shift when the sergeant who was parading us looked at him.

'Yogi, did I see you having a haircut on duty yesterday?'

'I don't know Sergeant, did you?'

'Yes, I did, you don't go for haircuts on duty. Understand?'

'It grows on duty sergeant.'

'You're not on duty all the time.'

'I didn't have it all cut off.'

The sergeant did not reply. Yogi's cards were marked.

It was the procedure that officers on foot patrol would go to a police box and 'ring in'. The officer would then make an entry in the log in the police box. On one occasion Yogi did not make his 4.00am ring, and at 5.30am the matter became more serious, with officers out searching his beat without success. At 6.00am the night duty relief had returned to Poplar Police Station.

At about 6.10am the telephone rang in the small reserve room at the nick, and a PC answered the phone. 'Poplar double one, one three. Police Station Poplar.' The officer pressed the headset against his head. 'I'm sorry, Sir, could you please speak up, I can't hear you.'

He looked round to the surrounding officers and indicated to keep the noise down. 'Yes, Sir, that's a little better, please can you tell me your name.'

Silence, the PC screwed his face in a quizzical manner. 'Please try to avoid whispering… okay, you're in a phone box… and your name, Sir? It's Yogi!'

'Put that through to me,' the Station Officer bellowed. The phone call was transferred to the phone on his desk. 'Where the hell are you, Yogi?' The sergeant's face was now turning a bright red. 'South-bleedin'-end, what the hell are you doing in Southend?'

There was a long pause, as the sergeant listened. 'Bullshit, my arse, you were carrying out an observation, you've never carried out an observation in your bleedin' life. Make your own way back here.'

There was a further plea from Yogi.

'Piss off, there is no chance of me sending a car for you.' With that the phone was slammed down.

Yogi did return, with his tale. 'At about 2.30am I was walking around the top of the ground when I saw two guys climbing into the railway sidings. They were obviously up to no good, so I climbed into a railway carriage to watch them. They vanished out of my sight. I sat there silently ready to pounce if and when they returned. I don't know if it was the warmth of the carriage or what but I must have dozed off for a few seconds, and then there was one almighty crash and I fell off the seat onto the floor. I jumped up, and it was then I realized they were shunting the carriages. The two guys must have been railway workers. The next thing I was on my way to Southend. I got off at the station and tried to avoid the local Old Bill. That's when I phoned you lot.'

We all looked in total disbelief as he tried to convince us his story was true.

'What went wrong Yogi? Didn't your alarm go off?'

It later transpired that a PC had discovered Yogi's night duty custom of going to the sidings for a couple of hours sleep in the empty carriages. Part of his night duty equipment was a travel alarm clock in a nice little folding case. He carried this in his tunic pocket. During the night he would take off his tunic and hang it on a peg on the wall, and then have his meal in the canteen. While away from the tunic someone readjusted the time settings making, the alarm go off at 5.55am, which meant Yogi would have had to run back to the nick to book off. This time when it went off, Yogi was in a sound sleep on his way to Southend.

Two months later Yogi transferred to a County Police Force.

After a month of learning beats I was then out on my own. London was still suffering from very bad fog. Visibility in daylight was frequently down to ten yards and, as soon as darkness fell this dropped considerably. I was walking towards the Blackwall Tunnel. As I approached the police post I could see the light was flashing, indicating there was a message to be answered. I opened the metal door and picked up the phone. The operator at Limehouse Police Station told me to go to Canning Town Bridge, where a car had broken down and was likely to cause an accident. I walked past the docks to where the car was. My greatcoat was covered by a white deposit of frozen fog. I arrived at the car, a large Rover, and at the front a man was bent down over the fog light.

'What's the problem?'

He looked up. 'Just adjusting the lights officer.'

'Oh, I see just broken down have we?'

'Yes, just this minute.'

'No you haven't, this car's been here for…' I never got another word out. He was gone. I chased after him but he was soon lost in the fog.

First lesson – hold on to your prisoner.

I walked back towards the abandoned car. I was totally dejected, I had lost my first 'body'. Oh, well, back to the car and direct traffic round it. After a short walk, getting my breath back and spitting the black filth out of my mouth, I arrived back at the car. The passenger's door was wide open, with a pair of legs sticking out, toes pointing upwards. I couldn't believe my luck! There was a man underneath the dashboard, stealing the radio. Without saying a word I drew my truncheon and caught hold of one of his legs and lifted them up towards the car roof.

'What the fu…'

'I am arresting you for stealing, for stealing a car radio. You are not obliged to say anything, but anything you do say will be taken down in writing and may be given in evidence.' I couldn't get the words out quick enough. Later I found it easier to say 'You're nicked,' it was a lot easier and the 'client' understood it better.

'OK, just let my bleedin' leg go, you're doin' my back in.'

'OK, but don't try and run.' I slowly let his leg down. He struggled up and sat on the passenger's seat.' He was aged about 45 years and six feet tall. I had a grip of his arm with one hand and was brandishing the truncheon in the other. 'If you even think of running this is going over your nut, understand?'

'Yes, OK, guvnor. It's only a poxy bleedin' wireless, not the bleedin' crown jewels.' And with that we walked through the fog, over the bridge and into 41 Box, where we waited for the van. He was a very pleasant fellow and stood talking to me about his time in Glasgow during the war.

I was like a dog with two tails. My first arrest!

In those days, constables took all their prisoners to court the following morning at 10.00am and were responsible for presenting the case to the magistrate. In the rear of the court was a holding area where you waited with your prisoner. Frequently, the prisoner would deny having been in trouble with the police beforehand. There was one telephone in the holding area that was a direct line to the Criminal Records Office at Scotland Yard. When it rang, someone would answer it and call out the name of the prisoner. If it was your prisoner, you would struggle through the crowd and then scribble down his record for court, if and when he was found or pleaded guilty. It was a pretty chaotic system, but it worked. Prior to coming to court, I had spent time going through my evidence over and over again in my room at the Section House. It was still going through my head as I stood waiting with my prisoner. Then I heard the name of my prisoner being called out by a PC holding the phone above his head. After some effort, I reached the telephone and started to write down the information, making sure I got everything 'spot on'. The phone was taken from my hand by an 'aide to CID' that then helped guide me through the chaos. I was so grateful to him. That young aide was Graham Melvin from the nick at Poplar, who had assisted me throughout the time we were stationed there.

Graham was a methodical and first-class CID officer. He went on to solve many major crimes throughout his service and retired as Chief Superintendent.

Poplar was a busy station, being situated on East India Dock Road next to the junction with Chrisp Street, where the local market was. I enjoyed my time there. In my first two years I had hundreds of arrests, including people for shop-breaking and various other criminal offences. One thing that was instilled into us was we were not allowed to permit any groups of youths to congregate on street corners.

I was riding my push bike on night duty when I came across a group of six youths standing on a street corner. After three warnings, they still remained. I telephoned for 'the van'. It duly arrived and the six yobs were scooped up and taken to the Police station, where they were charged with obstruction.

The next afternoon they appeared in front of Mr Cecil Campion, one of the Magistrates at Thames Court. Two things Cecil did not like were yobs and court timewasters - after all he had a train to catch!

The six accused appeared in front of him. I gave my evidence. Their solicitor cross-examined me.

'Officer, you have told the court that you told the accused to "Move along"?'

'Correct.'

'How many times did you say "Move along", Officer?'

'Three times, Sir.'

'What did you say on each occasion?'

There was then a heavy sigh from Mr Campion as he pulled up the sleeve of his jacket and looked at his watch.

'Move along.'

'On each occasion?'

'Yes, Sir'

'Tell the court what you said on the alleged last occasion.'

A heavy 'puff' came from Mr Campion, as he leant over and removed his handkerchief from his trouser pocket and gave his nose a hearty blow.

'Move along, or you will all be arrested.'

'Ah, now we are getting nearer the truth, aren't we Officer? I put it to you, Officer, that your actual words were, "FUCK OFF, OR YOU'RE ALL NICKED!"'

Mr Campion leant across his desk and in a stage whisper spoke to his Clerk, Mr S French. 'And it's a pity they didn't. They would not have been here today.' He flopped back into his high chair, exhaling as he did so. His left elbow sunk into the padded armrest as his hand cupped his head and he stared at the floor.

'Mr Gordon-Smythe, is this line of questioning getting us any where?'

'No further questions, Sir.'

With that Cecil sat up, bent over and rested his arms on his desk. 'I find each and every one of you guilty. If you choose to hang around street corners, obstructing the highway, that's your decision. Let me tell you the footway is part of the highway, and if you obstruct it you will be arrested if you pay no heed to the officer when he tells you to move on. One pound each!'

With that he pushed his chair back, picked up his walking stick and limped out of court.

What a difference today we see on our streets. Mr and Mrs Average walking off the pavement to walk round a crowd of yobs, afraid that they may be assaulted. I see police officers asking to be excused as they attempt to walk along the Queen's highway through a group of yobs. Why?

I stopped and searched hundreds of people under Section 66 of the Metropolitan Police Act. Likewise, I arrested people for being suspected persons under the old 'sus law'. The majority of them pleaded Guilty at court. The streets were safer. We didn't have 'muggings' (I prefer to call them by their correct name: robbery). Prior to that, we used to call the culprits highwaymen, and we know what happened to them. Now there's a thought!

As a young constable I walked into the charge room at Limehouse Police Station, where sitting on the bench were two old Chinese men complete with ponytails and little ribbon bows on the end. They had been arrested for possession of opium by the Drug Squad; two detectives dressed in trench coats and trilby hats. The Drug Squad in the early '60s and before consisted of a handful of older detectives whose main job was to inspect the drugs register in local chemist shops. The Chinese were more or less arrested by appointment, charged and taken to court where they received a nominal fine. Drugs as we know them now were unheard of then. We were never shown any type of drug at training school. Now, the streets are awash with them. In most city centres you don't have to walk far to see drug deals taking place. Now we have senior police officers and politicians trying to legalize it! We in Britain have, over the years, had a culture of 'If you can't beat it legalize it'.

I was loving every minute of my chosen career, I never once hated going to work. In the middle of 1965 the Metropolitan Police decided to introduce Velocette lightweight motorcycles to the Inner London Divisions. This included H Division. The motorcycles were soon nicknamed 'Noddy bikes' after the children's TV character. I applied to go on the motorcycle test at the Driving School at Hendon and was successful in getting through the course. It was not long before I was posted to lightweight motorcycle duties, covering Limehouse and Poplar sub-divisions.

As Christmas approached, and with it the amount of break-ins into shops, I applied to go on a patrol from 6.00pm until 2.00am, thus covering the times when other officers were in having refreshments and shifts were being changed. This was a new concept on the division. The Superintendent approved my application and I was let loose on the streets! I was having considerable success in arresting people for stealing motor cars and shop-breaking etc.

A new type of telephone box had been introduced to London. These were known as STD (Subscriber Trunk Dialling). Their cash boxes were fairly easy to break into. The head of the then Post Office announced in Parliament that the losses from these boxes were in excess of £4.5 million a year.

On a winter's night at 12.10am I was in West Ferry Road heading towards the Isle of Dogs. As I rode past a telephone box on my right hand side I noticed two males inside. I stopped and pulled the bike onto the stand. As I started to cross the road towards them, the one holding the door open ran off. I ran to the box. The other male, who was bent down inside, got up and ran towards me. In his hand he was carrying a red metal crowbar. He raised the crowbar above his head and I took the full force of it on my motorcycle helmet. I fell to my knees, dazed, but saved from serious injury by my 'Noddy' helmet. I got up, but he ran off, stopped, turned round and threw the crowbar at me. It bounced off the pavement with a shower of sparks and hit me on the chest. With that he was off.

We had no means of communication, other than our police whistles. The instruction manual issued to police stated that if assistance was required we should blow our whistle in three short blasts. Failing that, we should flash our police issue torch in the direction of the nearest police officer. Unfortunately, neither of these methods was possible as the closest police officers were in the police canteen at Limehouse Police Station, and I was out of puff. I stopped a passing taxi and he used his radio to called for assistance.

Within a short period of time the local area car arrived and I spilled out my story to the driver and crew. 'There were two geezers, one black; I don't what the other one was. They were screwing the phone box. The black geezer's wearing a full-length black leather coat. They both ran off in that direction.' As I spoke, I indicated towards the Eastern Pub at East India Dock Road.

I got back onto the motorcycle and rode towards the Rotherhithe Tunnel. I was determined I was going to have this geezer if it was the last thing I was going to do. It nearly was.

A taxi was pulling up at the traffic lights at the Rotherhithe Tunnel and I pulled up next to the driver. He put down his window. It could not have been raining harder and I was soaked through. 'You haven't seen a black geezer wearing a black leather coat, have you mate?'

The driver continued to look out of his window and spoke out of the corner of his mouth. 'He's in the back mate.'

I looked over my shoulder and there was 'my man' on the floor of the cab. As I tried to pull the motorcycle onto the stand, he opened the passenger door and ran out across the road into Whitehorse Lane. I chased him round the corner. As he was running along the pavement, splashing through the puddles. I bumped the bike up onto the pavement and accelerated after him. As I got close to him he stopped, and I hit him with the full force of the bike. He fell to the ground. The bike fell over, with me under it. As I was struggling to my feet, he caught me with a full force of his boot on my chest. I rolled over and got up, attempting to draw my truncheon from my truncheon pocket which was sewn into the right hand side of my uniform trousers. Not an easy task when in full-uniform, covered with a motorcycle coat buttoned between your legs, and wearing a crash helmet. I noticed something in his right hand. It was a pistol. There was then one almighty fight, and I eventually fell unconscious. It wasn't supposed to be like this, I was supposed to win!

The next thing I remember was my head resting on the rain-soaked negligee of a beautiful 18-year-old female. I thought I had arrived in heaven. Two Chinese from the local Chinese restaurant looked down at me, the rain dripping off their noses.

'You okay, policeman?'

I couldn't speak. My head was spinning from the fight and trying to focus on the view four inches from my nose!

'You okay, policeman?'

What healthy young man wouldn't be okay lying on a wet pavement, with his head resting on a blonde eighteen-year-old's lap?

'It… yes, yes, I'm okay, did you see the man, the man I was fighting with?'

'No, we telephoned for an ambulance to take you hospital.'

With that I could hear the bells of the police cars as they came to my assistance. They must have been close, the bells could only be heard from about twenty-five yards on a good day.

The car stopped next to me, the crew got out and ran over. I could hear the sound of the car radio as they ran towards me, leaving the car doors open.

'Oh shit, not you again 321! What are we going to do with you?'

'It was the black guy who did the phone box up the road. He's still wearing the black leather coat. He's got a pistol,' I said.

As I was led to the ambulance doors I could hear the radio operator sending a message. 'MP from Hotel-2. We have found the PC. He is going to the London Hospital. The suspect is a black male, aged about twenty years. He is wearing a black leather coat and is believed to be armed with a pistol. I repeat, he is believed to be armed with a pistol. Last seen running towards Arbour Square Police Station.'

I was put into the ambulance and taken to the London Hospital. After examination I was discharged and collected by the area car. While making our way back to the nick we received a radio message stating that my suspect was now in custody at Arbour Square Police Station.

As I walked into the charge room, I looked over and there sitting on the bench, with his elbows on his knees and his head in his hands, was my man. His leather coat was lying on the floor. Three constables were standing next to him. Lying on the charge room table was my truncheon, I hadn't even missed it.

'Where did you find him?' I asked.

Colin Bulley, a local police constable based at Arbour Square Police Station, picked up the story. 'All of the guys at the nick had turned out to look for him. As I came onto a piece of waste ground just off Commercial Road I saw him standing in the dark. I challenged him and he immediately pulled a knife on me. I tried to reason with him, to no avail, he was set to have a go at me. I drew my truncheon and hit him. He dropped the knife and I overpowered and nicked him. Since he's been in the nick, he's been fighting like a caged tiger - haven't you my son?'

'What's your name mate?' I asked him, looking straight into his eyes.

'Piss off, I don't have to tell you anything.'

'Well, let me tell you something, arsehole. You are going to be charged with assault on police and screwing the telephone box on the Isle of Dogs. Where is the pistol you had?'

'You bunch of shit, I don't have to talk to you.'

The PCs looked at me in amazement. 'A gun, nobody told us about a gun.'

'Yes, a gun, he had a gun, didn't you? When I came round the corner at White Horse Lane, he had it in his right hand. It was a black pistol type thing.'

'One more time, where is the gun?' I asked.

found under the car after the telephone box incident. He looked at the gun, smiled, and said, 'Think yourself lucky I didn't use it on you.' I did.

It transpired that Hussein was sixteen and had numerous convictions. When he appeared at the Juvenile Court in relation to my case, he was wearing handcuffs as he entered the court. Mrs Mary Stuart was the Magistrate. 'Why is this boy in handcuffs? I am not having this in MY court, take them off,' she said.

'Mam, this youth has escaped from custody and has been involved in serious assaults on two police officers where a firearm was used. More serious charges will follow.' The officer's voice was drowned out by the Magistrate. 'Take these handcuffs off this youth now!' The key was produced and the officers unscrewed the lock on the handcuffs.

'That's better. Now young man, do you understand why you are here?'

'No lady, I have been beaten up by the police and...'

'No, you must answer a few simple questions first... Do you...'

'Fuck you all!' and with that Hussein leapt forward onto the table in front of the Magistrate. She in turn did some form of 'back flip' and was out of the court shouting, 'Handcuff him, handcuff him.' Hussein was restrained and duly handcuffed.

After a few minutes, the magistrate reappeared in court and told Hussein in no uncertain terms that he would be remanded in custody. He was taken screaming and fighting from the court.

He was remanded in custody and eventually stood trial at the Central Criminal Court. He pleaded guilty to the offences and was sentenced to eight years' imprisonment.

This was the first time in my life that I had met someone who I believe was really bad, and had no respect for anyone. It would not be the last time I would meet 'bad' people; little did I think some would be serving police officers.

After his release from prison Hussein carried on a life of crime. On one occasion he cut a jeweller's throat while breaking into the man's property. He was jailed for this, and while in prison carried out a serious assault on another prisoner.

Packman and Connell received the British Empire Medal for Gallantry. I received a Commissioner's Commendation.

For me, despite all, it was back to duty doing the job I loved.

FIVE

FLY-TIPPER

During the reconstruction of Poplar and the building of the new Blackwall Tunnel under the Thames, lorry drivers were making lots of money removing rubble from the construction areas and depositing it at authorised sites. Many of these drivers were self-employed and paid by the load. This encouraged certain drivers to fly-tip, even dropping their load in the middle of side streets, totally blocking the road and costing the local council to clear up.

I was on early turn on the 'Noddy' when I came across a tipper lorry driving down a side road. The driver had the bed of the lorry up and was spewing the contents on the road as he drove along. I pulled alongside him and waved him down. He stopped and jumped down from his cab. He was in his early twenties with a boyish-looking face. Somehow he did not fit into the mould of a typical lorry driver. He removed a pair of industrial gloves from his hands; hands that were more suited to a surgeon than a lorry driver. I couldn't imagine this guy in a transport café with these hands wrapped round a mug of tea. No, not him, he was more suited to fairy cakes and bone china!

'Oh, dear, Officer, I didn't realise my rear had gone up, I'm ever so sorry. Please forgive me.'

As I looked at him I thought, this is not the first time his rear's gone up, and I wasn't thinking of his lorry's tailgate.

I reported him and issued him with a notice to produce his insurance and driving licence. He thanked me and climbed back into his cab and drove off. I had a gut feeling that things were not right, and under the circumstances I decide to follow him at a distance. After about four miles he pulled in and stopped near the public baths in Bethnal Green. I stopped behind the lorry and walked to the front as he jumped down the cab. On seeing me he hit the ground running. He vanished into a side alleyway. A woman pushing a pram towards me pointed to an eight-foot wall which surrounded a row of Victorian terraced houses.

'He's over there,' she said, and with that she continued on her way.

'Cheers.' I scrambled onto the top of the wall and sat, one leg either side. Below me and leaning against the wall, his hands on his knees, was my man. Then the farce started. Curtains twitched within the house whose garden he was in. He looked up.

'Oh, no, not you again!'

'Get up here, you're nicked my son!' and with that I drew my truncheon.

'Bollocks, you can't touch me in here.'

'Get up.'

'No, I'm safe in here.'

I'm thinking to myself, this dickhead thinks he's in some form of sanctuary!

'Get up here and don't be such a prat!'

'No, I'm not coming up there for you.' It was at this stage that his effeminate voice became noticeable.

'Get up here, this is your last chance!'

'No, no, you're, you're going to beat me up.'

'No, I'm not. Now get up here, NOW!'

'Put that bit of wood away, then I'll come up, promise.'

I put the truncheon back in my pocket. 'Right you, up.' And with that he ran at the wall and caught my outstretched arm. I pulled him onto the top of the wall. We sat facing each other.

'Now, I'm going down first, OK?'

'Yes officer, I'm sorry for all the trouble,' and with that I jumped down. He brought his leg over the wall and started to swing down. As he did so he kicked me on the side of the head. Fortunately, I had hold of his other leg and we both fell to the ground, where we rolled around exchanging blows. Eventually, I got his arm up his back and marched him off to a nearby Police Box. Once inside I telephoned for 'urgent assistance' and with that he was off again, punching, scratching, spitting and screaming. He then got hold of my tie and started to throttle me. The inside of a police box could barely hold two people. I was trying to free myself to no avail. He was screaming like a banshee. I reached down with my right hand and grabbed hold of his nuts and squeezed as hard as I could. He let go of my tie. I then gave him a 'Glasgow kiss' (a head butt) between his eyes. He fell back, blood running down his face. I had never done this before; I don't know who got the biggest fright, him or me. I thought I had killed him.

'OK, that's it, I've had enough.' He slumped against the wall; both of us were totally exhausted.

Alpha Seven, the City of London's area car, arrived and PC Martin, the tallest policeman I had ever seen, got out and assisted me. His brother, Pete, a Metropolitan Police officer and every bit as tall, died some years later while rescuing passengers from the sea during the Zeebrugge ferry disaster. Pete had been a passenger on the ship when the disaster happened.

We bundled the prisoner into the police car and took him back to the local station. He still refused to give any information about himself. After about ten minutes Detective Sergeant Trevor Lloyd-Hughes walked into the charge room, his face beaming.

'Well, 321, what have we got this time?' Trevor, a resident in the Section House, was known to me and had dealt with other arrests I had been involved with. Why was he here - he didn't work at this nick?

I started to explain what had happened, when he interrupted. He looked over at the prisoner, who had refused to see a doctor. 'Hello Bobby.'

'I'm not Bobby!'

'Oh! Yes you are. Robert Buckley, your CRO number slips my mind. You live at...' with that he gave him his home address. Buckley's head dropped. Trevor looked at the station sergeant.

'Stick him down the cells and we will have a cup of tea. See you later, Bobby.'

We walked into the canteen and sat at a table.

'So you know him?'

'Oh, yes, I know him. In fact, our team has an interest in him and his friends. I think we should go and search his home address later.

Jim, don't mention to anyone about our interest in him, OK?'

'Yes, but can I ask who he is?'

'Yes, okay. Are you ready?'

I looked puzzled.

'He's one of Ronnie Kray's boyfriends, and the garden he was in?'

I was even more puzzled.

'That was number 178 Vallance Road, the home of the Kray twins, and to think two hours ago you were squeezing Ronnie Kray's boyfriend's bollocks!'

A few days after Buckley was convicted I received a postcard at the Section House. The writer congratulated me and finished by saying that naughty boys needed spanking. It was unsigned.

Much later, I learned that Trevor was part of the Kray Squad, gathering evidence for their successful conviction. I did not see Buckley again until after the arrest of the Kray 'Firm', when it was our duty to guard them throughout the trial. We were given one prisoner between two officers. On the first day of the committal hearing we escorted the prison van from Brixton Prison into the Station Yard at Bow Street Police Station. In the station yard we jumped out of our carrier and collected our prisoner to take to the cells. My prisoner on the first day was none other than Bobby Buckley.

'Ooh! PC Smith, it looks like I'm yours.' A comedian to the end.

He died in the Seventies from drug abuse.

SIX

THE NEW SPG

I applied for and was accepted into the newly-formed Special Patrol Group. I was posted to Three Unit, working out of the East End of London. We were sent wherever there was either a high level of crime, or where a major incident had occurred. The group consisted of three carriers, each carrying about ten officers. The press named us as the 'Blue Cobras'. Other groups called us 'Fascist Bastards' and yet again we were called 'The Elite'. The image put over was each and every officer was a one-man 'crimebuster'.

Nothing could have been further from the truth. There was one sergeant and about six PCs, who suffered from 'back problems', ie they could not get their backs off the seats of the carriers to deal with any incident. They came into their own when running the revenue-raising Tea Club or social events. To them, the SPG was just a job, a means of paying the mortgage. They earned their nickname The Gurkhas as they didn't take prisoners. Often, when new departments were formed within the service, senior officers saw a golden opportunity to recommend and offload idle and overconscientious officers.

Cash and Carry warehouses were just opening up around London and these officers 'expanded' the Tea Club into a mini-supermarket, selling everything from knickers to meat. 'You must place your meat orders by Thursday night!' So the notice in the office read. There was nothing dishonest in what they were doing, and they saved us a few bob. As young married men, we were grateful for any savings. The sales of knickers did not do too well after the first week. Apparently, wives were having problems caused by static electricity from the nylon. That line was discontinued!

I was paired up with 'Dixie' Dean. We worked well together and had numerous crime arrests throughout the Metropolitan Police district. On one occasion Dixie and I were in plainclothes working Soho. We had stopped to speak to one of the girls on the door of a clip joint in Peter Street. While talking to her, a man started to leave the club. He was having difficulty getting past the three of us. For some reason, he turned his back on Dixie and the girl opened his jacket to reveal the butt of a pistol sticking out of the waistband of his trousers. I did a double take; it was definitely a pistol. He nodded, indicating he wanted us to leave. I caught hold of Dixie's sleeve and we walked off.

When two police officers work well together, they don't have to say anything. They develop a sixth sense, no words have to be spoken. A nod or a certain look does it.

We walked round the corner. 'What was that all about?' Dixie asked.

'The geezer in the club door has got a shooter tucked in the top of his trousers.'

With that, 'the geezer' walked round the corner, and as he did so, we both hit him. He fell onto the pavement. Dixie pulled the man's arms above his head and as he did so his jacket fell open revealing the pistol. 'Grab it,' Dixie said.

I didn't have to be told twice. I pulled the gun out and put it on the pavement next to us. After a bit of a struggle the man was subdued. We subsequently discovered that the pistol was a replica and our prisoner was a London bus driver. We never did discover what his motive was. There was one thing for sure - if people were going to carry replica firearms, they would be putting their life in danger when they pointed them at anyone. A few years later this would become all too true - as I stood looking at the dead bodies of two youths on the floor of the Indian High Commission in London.

As a group, the SPG were involved in most of the major incidents in London including the Grosvenor Square riots of

1968 when thousands of people took to the streets to protest against the Vietnam War. These demonstrations were some of the most frightening I had ever attended. We were not equipped with any protective clothing or shields. The attitude at the Yard was: our police will police in the conventional manner, not like the foreign 'Johnnies' using tear gas and water cannons.

Our carriers were stationed behind Selfridges in Oxford Street. We listened on the police radio to the movement of the crowd as they progressed towards Grosvenor Square. We heard on the police radio that a police motorcyclist had been dragged from his bike and it had been set on fire. We rushed to the Square, where we were involved in fights until the early evening. Our instructions were to guard the American Embassy and stop any demonstrators getting onto the steps, and most of all into the Embassy. We were warned that should the crowd break through the Embassy doors we were to immediately disperse, as the US Marines inside would open fire with live rounds on the crowd. Fortunately, it never came to that, despite Tariq Ali and Vanessa Redgrave encouraging the demonstrators to 'advance'.

SEVEN

MEXICO AND LIVE SEX SHOWS

'Want to see a live sex show in a private room?'

It seemed that during the mid-Sixties every male on his own in Soho was being asked this question by Maltese immigrants who imported the con into London and found an easy way to make money from unsuspecting, sometimes only too willing punters. It was going on morning, noon and night. Their method was to loiter in Soho and watch potential punters, who would usually be looking into the windows of sex shops. Very few, if any, of the shows had live sex acts. The idea was to hook unsuspecting males into a room and take their money on the promise of some form of sex act. These guys were expert at getting the punter's particular interest, and then leading them to some unlit flat or empty club. They would relieve them of money and then take off, leaving the 'sucker' (the name used by the 'Malts' for their clients) sitting in an empty room waiting for his sexual fantasy to materialize.

On occasions when the sucker demanded to see the show commence before he parted with his money, heavies would arrive and they would relieve him of his money, usually giving him a hiding into the bargain. It could be argued that such suckers took their chances.

The conmen had been running this scam for years before it came to the attention of police. The suckers, after they had been rolled, realized what fools they had been and very seldom reported the incident to police. If and when they did, it was always reported by them as a pick-pocketing incident that had gone wrong. This covered the loss of the money when they 'reported' the incident to their wives.

It reached such proportions that it was pushing up the crime figures in the area, and also affecting tourism. Number Three Unit of the SPG, led by Inspector Les David, was called in. We were briefed, and then, all in plainclothes (with the exception of the drivers and a radio operator), set off in the carriers and were dropped off near the area. I was one of the people chosen to be the fall guy. The sucker! I would dress in a blazer, flannels, white shirt and wearing my old school tie. I carried a rolled umbrella - with my truncheon inside - completing the 'props'.

Harrison Marks was a theatrical photographer who also did studies of the female figure. He had a studio in Gerrard Street. In the window he exhibited some of his photographs of black-and-white studies of the female form. I would walk down the street, stop with a 'lost' look on my face, stand at the window and drool over the pictures. It only took a few minutes before I got a bite.

'Want to see a show, Sir?'

At this point I went into the full Glasgow patter.

'Oh, Jees, whit, whit's your game?' I would then take two steps back in shock.

'No, don't worry, it's okay.'

'Don't worry? Ah nearly shit ma sel.'

'Where are you from?'

'Glesga, why whit's it got tae do wi you?'

'Where is this, Glesga?

'Scotland.'

'Oh, Glasgow.'

'Aye, Glesga. Why, what's it got to dae wi you?'

'Scotland is very beautiful, I had girl from Scotland she was very nice.'

'Aye great, whit do you want?' I kept glancing at the pictures in the window.

'You like the picture?

'Aye, they're OK, but yi cannae see much. You know what I mean?'

'You like to see something better?'

'Whit do you mean, better?'

'A nice woman getting shagged by a man.'

Now, the amazed and shocked look comes on my face.

'Whit!'

'Yes, on a little stage, you can sit and watch.'

'Yir kiddin!'

'No, no. No jokey, come I take you and…' with that he took my elbow and directed me down the street.

'Hey, jist a minute.'

'Here, here come in the doorway and we talk.' I was ushered into a doorway. 'We got to be careful, the police, you know, we are not supposed to do this.'

'Whit Polis, ah don't want any trouble.'

'No trouble, my Scotland friend, listen. It's ten pounds to see the show and you can have black, Chinese, or Swedish. They are all beautiful girls and the man will screw them and you can sit and watch have a little drink.'

'Whit, all for ten quid?'

'Only ten pound, my Scotland friend.'

'Aye, OK. Where is it?'

There was an air of excitement in my voice; he loved it.

'Just down the road, you gotta the money?'

'Oh aye, I've got the money, but 'am no givin' it to you here, 'am no daft!'

'No, we go down to the little club, follow me it's not far my Scotland friend.'

He then walked into the doorway of premises a couple of doors away. He looked up and down the street.

'It's OK, you come now.'

And with that I was ushered down the stairs.

If this happened to me once, it happened at least twenty times. It was always the same story.

Needless to say, there was never a show. Once I was in the club I would drop a hint about police and the man would run off into the arms of the team who were waiting outside. I would then arrest him for AFP (Attempted False Pretences). Frequently, when searched they would be carrying an offensive weapon.

When inquiries were made at the police station into their background it was often found that some were wanted for other criminal offences. The Magistrates at the court always sent them to the Crown Court for sentence, and frequently they were given at least twelve months' imprisonment. It all but stopped this type of crime in the West End. Longer sentences do work. In today's climate they would have most likely been given Community Service.

On one such occasion I was 'clipped', and after having gone through the usual Glasgow routine was taken down a metal staircase and into a dimly lit cellar bar.

'Just a-sit down and the show will soon start. I'll just get the beautiful young lady ready. Just give me the £10. You're lucky, you are the only one in today, a private show for the Scottish man.'

I could see the look of anticipation on his face as he hooked another mug.

I looked up into his sleazy face as I reached into my pocket for my wallet.

'How long does the show last?'

'As a long as you want to stay, my friend.'

'Okay. It's just that I can't be too long as I am having my grub at West End Central Police...'

Before I could finish the sentence he was off through the door, onto the metal staircase and scampering upstairs. I sat still, there was no point in chasing after him. There was a reception party waiting upstairs. After a few moments he reappeared between Inspector David and Dixie Dean.

The lights were put on to reveal a dirty hovel of a place. There were so many stains on the carpet it looked like a 'skid pan'. In the corner was a grey filing cabinet. On top of a desk was a cash register and behind the so-called stage, tawdry curtains were hanging on string. They, like the rest of the place, were covered in thick dust and the room reeked of dried urine and stale beer. We pulled up a chair and let the 'Malt' sit down.

'Let us introduce ourselves, I am Inspector David, this is PC Dean, and I believe you have met PC Smith.'

'My Scottish friend,' he tried to smile.

'Can we do a deal? I have £100 in my pocket and I can get more. Please no prison… I have two children and my wife is…'

'Dying?' I finished the sentence for him.

'Tell me, is the money clean money?'

His eyes lit up.

'Yes, its clean money, I can get more, but please, no prison.'

'No, £100 is enough to stick up your arse at once. Thank you!'

Mr David interrupted. 'I will forget your last remark. I don't know which police officers you have dealt with in the past, but don't come that old nonsense with us, we are not interested.'

Our prisoner's head dropped down as he stared at the floor.

'I'm sorry, no hard feelings?'

'Who owns the club?'

He looked at me, his slimy smile had gone. 'I don't know. I just use it when it's empty.'

'Where are the artists?'

He looked up at Inspector David. 'You know, Sir, they no here.'

As we talked, Inspector David was trying to open the filing cabinet. He looked round. 'What's in here, mate?'

'I no know, I think it is empty.' He held out his out-stretched hands.

'If you don't know, how come you know it's empty? Give me the key.'

'I don't have no key.' He then looked at Inspector David and added, 'Honestly.'

We searched him; he didn't have a key.

Inspector David and Dixie pulled the filing cabinet away from the wall. Taped to the back of it was an axe. Inspector David pulled the cabinet round and, smiling, looked at the Malt.

'Well, what do you know, I've just found the key!'

With that he pulled the axe off the back of the Cabinet.

'Here, open it,' he handed him the axe as we surrounded the Malt.

'Now use this key.'

The guy looked at the axe.

'I get big trouble.' He looked at me.

'Don't worry, we won't tell anyone,' David said.

He then set about the cabinet trying to prize open the drawers. Eventually, there was a crash and the lock gave way. We took the axe from him and searched through the cabinet. He had told the truth on this occasion; it was empty.

Over in the corner next to the door was the cash register. I looked into the drawer. It too was empty. I pulled the drawer completely out and looked in the space. There was nothing in the recess. As I was putting the drawer back in position, I noticed something taped to the back. I removed the six inches of gaffer tape which was holding the object. It was a key.

'Ah, look what I've found, the key to the cabinet.'

I took it over to the cabinet. It didn't fit. The shank of the key had the letters 'LY54' stamped on it. The other parts of the letters had been filed off.

The Malt denied all knowledge of it, and he was taken to West End Central Police Station where he was charged. The next day he appeared at Marlborough Street Magistrates' Court. He pleaded guilty and was sent up the road for sentence.

The key was burning a hole in my pocket. I needed to find the lock, and most of all I wanted to know what secrets it protected. I visited banks, stations, left luggage areas etc, all without success.

Eventually, after days of searching, a locksmith recognized it as a foreign-manufactured key and thought it may belong to a safety deposit box. After days of walking round the West End, I eventually ended up in the British European Airways office in Bond Street. The receptionist was very helpful and took the key from me and went to the rear office. She returned after a short time and handed it back.

'I'm sorry. I've shown it to the rest of the staff, it doesn't mean anything to any of them.'

'Excuse me, did you say you were a policeman?' I looked round and standing next to me was a woman aged about sixty. Her dress indicated to me that she was not short of a few bob.

'Yes, can I help you?' and with that I showed her my warrant card.

'May I see the key? I think I may be able to help you.'

'Yes, certainly.' I handed her the key.

She studied it for a few seconds and then put it on the counter in front of her. She then opened her expensive handbag and brought out some keys. She searched through the bunch selected one and held it up.

'Is this what you're looking for?'

I took the bunch and looked at the embossing on the key. It read, 'ORLY 52'.

I looked at her, a look of bewilderment on my face. My stomach churned with excitement.

'It's my left luggage locker at Orly Airport, in Paris.'

I could have kissed her.

I returned to West End Central Police Station and got the telephone number for Orly Airport. Eventually, I spoke to what I believed was a French cop, but it was a hopeless task.

'No French… No English… Sorry… Pardon.'

That was the end of that conversation.

That night I was on a 6.00pm to 2.00am shift. At mealtime in the Section House I relayed the events of the day to Inspector David, who had a wealth of knowledge on police procedure.

'Oh, that's easy. We send a message via Interpol. Get me a copy of GO' (General Orders, the Metropolitan Police's bigger Bible).

I returned a few minutes later carrying the book. Inspector David thumbed his way through the pages. 'Right, here we are, Interpol messages. Who's authorized to send them?' He read slowly through the paragraphs. 'Yes, as I thought, I've got the rank to send it. Let's find a typewriter.'

The report was duly sent off. Being keen, I was looking for a reply the next day. About two months later I was sitting in the dock at Bow Street Magistrates' Court next to the infamous Kray twins. Halfway through the morning session the oak-panelled door in number one court opened about six inches and I saw Inspector David looking directly at me. He nodded at a piece of paper in his hand. The note made its way round the court and eventually arrived with me.

It was addressed '561CO' (my number). I opened it and read it:

'The ACC wants to see us at one-thirty at CO.'

David and I got into the Hillman Minx and drove to Scotland Yard.

'What have you been up to?' he asked.

'Nothing guv, honestly.'

'Well, he wants to see me and you. What have we done?'

We were shown into Peter Brodie's office.

'Come in, shut the door and sit down. Do you know why you're here, Inspector David, PC Smith?'

'No, sir,' we answered in harmony.

'Well, let me ask you what the Special Patrol Group has got to do with a political assassination in Mexico?'

'I'm afraid I don't understand, Sir,' David said.

'You don't understand? How do you think I'm supposed to understand when I receive a telex like this?'

He put on his spectacles and read the text, looking over the rim.

'For the attention of Inspector L. David, Metropolitan Police London, Unit Three Special Patrol Group. At your request, we have opened the security box number 54 at Orly Airport. We found: One Mauser Machine Pistol, two hundred rounds of 9mm ammunition suitable for the Mauser machine pistol, two hand grenades, one pair of binoculars, one pair of running shoes, one thermos flask and two thousand French Francs. Ballistic tests have been carried out on the Mauser Machine Pistol. It is confirmed that this weapon was used in a political assassination in Mexico. We await your further instructions.'

The ACC slowly removed his spectacles and put the telex message on his desk. He leant back in his chair.

'Well?'

'Ah, that message, I had almost forgotten about that. You see Jock arrested a Maltese male for AFP... Sex shows...'

The rest of the conversation seemed to vanish in some form of misty dream as I looked at the ACC's face as he stared in disbelief.

I 'awakened' as he leant forward and said in a I-don't-believe-a word-of it-tone, 'Where is this key now?'

I undid the button of the breast pocket of my uniform and

removed my whistle chain. Attached to it was 'the key'. I removed it and handed it to him. He took it, examined it and looked up.

'I'll keep this, thank you gentlemen. I will deal with this matter from now on.'

I wrote in my pocket book: RECEIVED FROM P.C. 561C.O. SMITH ONE KEY WITH THE WORDING, 'LY 54' THEREON.

I handed the pocket book over. He signed it, with eyebrows raised.

Both of us walked down the corridor in silence and stopped at the lift. Inspector David looked at me.

'A political assassination...'

I looked at him, 'All from an AFP.'

We both burst out laughing.

'It looks as if we are going to France and Mexico, Guv'nor.'

Inspector David looked at me, 'Jock, there is more chance of a man on the Moon than us going there. I liked the bit of you getting a receipt in your pocket book.'

Two years later, on 21st July, 1969, Neil Armstrong landed on the Moon. We never did go to France or Mexico. Neither did we ever hear of the outcome.

EIGHT

HARRY ROBERTS

On Friday, 12th August, 1966, at approximately 3 o'clock, I was in the canteen at Harold Scott House along with several other officers. On the rear of the chairs hung our uniform jackets and ties. Radio Caroline was playing on the large Pye radio in the corner. Night duty officers had come downstairs from their bedrooms and were having their breakfast. The morning papers were lying on the tables.

I had just come down from my room and was about go to work with the SPG for the 6.00pm to 2.00am shift, starting at Old Street Police Station.

It was just a normal day.

We were interrupted by a uniform PC running into the canteen cap in hand, 'Foxtrot One One has been shot up!'

We all knew Foxtrot 11 was the local Q Car on F Division, but nobody could fully take in the message.

There was silence in the canteen, PCs looked up, there was a pause, and then the PC shouted across the canteen, 'They're all dead… the whole crew have been shot dead!'

'What?' someone asked.

'They're all dead. They've all been killed, they are all fucking dead, fucking shot!

He turned round and ran back to the yard, but stopped and shouted, 'It's on the radio on the area car in the station yard.' We all ran into the yard, where the area car with its doors wide open was already surrounded by police officers, from Guv'nors to PCs.

It soon became clear that the local area car on F Division had received a radio message from Scotland Yard to go to Braybrook Street, a residential area outside Wormwood Scrubs Prison. On their arrival they were met by a horrific scene.

We stood round the police car listening in disbelief. This had never happened in the Metropolitan Police, or any force within the United Kingdom. Villains didn't carry guns. Well, maybe a few, but shoot dead three police officers? It was unthinkable.

There were so many radio transmissions, but the one I will remember most of all was the operator saying, 'NO! NO! We do not require an ambulance. They are all dead.'

A further message was transmitted: 'The suspects are believed to be driving a car, registration number PGT 726.'

We scribbled this number down on scrap paper or on the palms of our hands and rushed back into the canteen. We then rushed to Old Street Police Station, where the engines of the carriers were already running, the doors open.

Officers stood around waiting for the message that we were fully expecting. 'MP to all uniform units REGROUP. Map reference XX2.' This location was Shepherd's Bush. REGROUP was a Home Office instruction to get the newly-formed Special Patrol Group to a location as quickly as possible.

At Shepherd's Bush Section House more than 200 officers gathered in a large assembly room. There was total silence. Chief Superintendent David Powis made his way onto the raised platform.

'I have just come from the mortuary, where I have seen the bodies of our three colleagues.'

He paused. 'The crew of Foxtrot, One One. I have never seen a sight like it… Detective Sergeant Christopher Head was shot in the back. Detective Constable Wombwell was shot through the left eye. PC Geoffrey Fox, the driver, was shot through the left temple.'

He paused again and continued.

'This was a cold-blooded execution of these three officers, doing what we believe was a routine stop. Details are sparse at the moment, although it would appear there were two or three people involved in the shooting. They had at least two handguns. We will keep you posted as more information comes in. It's likely that they have dumped this vehicle somewhere locally. We want this vehicle. We do not want any heroics. We cannot afford another officer killed or injured in this inquiry. Each carrier will carry authorized shots. We must all put our best effort into this. We will be working very long hours, but we will get there. We are going to start by doing a beat sweep of the area. Maps will be made available. Good luck lads and ladies.'

We all shuffled out. There was none of the banter that we usually had after briefings.

The car had to be found: it was the key to the whole investigation.

People were stopped, cars were searched, and door-to-door inquiries were made, all without success. Coppers are a moaning lot, but I can honestly say there were no moans on this job, everyone wanted to catch the people responsible.

We received our instructions, and boarded our carriers. One by one the surrounding streets were searched with no results. This continued throughout the weekend.

Over the next couple of days further details of the murders came to light.

Bryan Deacon, a security guard, had been listening to the many BBC broadcasts appealing for witnesses.

It had been thought that two men were involved, but Deacon knew better and he provided the first clues. He had been going to visit relatives near Braybrook Street just after 3.00pm on the day of the murders and had seen a car being driven in a crazy manner away from the murder scene. He had seen three men in the car. The registered owner of the vehicle was eventually traced after a long physical search of the registration records at County Hall. It belonged to a John Edward Witney, who was living in a basement flat in Paddington. Officers rushed to his flat where, under questioning, he claimed to have sold his car that afternoon to a man outside a pub. His flat was searched for weapons, but none were found. He was locked up at Shepherd's Bush Police Station, where he stuck to his story that he had sold the car for £15. Nobody believed him, least of all his wife, who had watched him go to work everyday for the past few weeks despite the fact that he didn't have a job.

We were getting calls from all over London that the suspect car had been seen, but these leads were followed up without success. On the Saturday evening after the murder, Detective Superintendent Chitty, who was in charge of the murder inquiry, called a press conference and gave details of the cars involved. As a result of this appeal a member of the public phoned New Scotland Yard. On the previous day he had seen a Blue Standard Vanguard estate car being driven in Tinworth Street, in Lambeth, South London. There, in a lock-up garage, police officers found the killers' car. It was not long before they discovered that the garage was rented by Witney. Inside the vehicle were false number plates, three .38 calibre cartridges and part of a nylon stocking. This was a complete robbers' kit, and nobody had any doubt that the killings were down to Witney.

Detective Inspector Jack Slipper, one of the Metropolitan Police's nicest, and soon to become one of its most famous, officers was put on to the forensic inquiry. Tests were carried out on the car and Witney's fingerprints were found. His charge sheet as read to him was as follows:

> 'John Edward Witney, 36, unemployed of Fernhead Road, Paddington, you are charged that with others on Friday the 12th of August, 1966, at Braybrook Street, you did murder Christopher Tippett Head. That with others on the same day and place you murdered David Stanley Wombwell. That with others you murdered Geoffrey Roger Fox.'

Witney was fingerprinted and put in a cell on his own, his only contact with the outside world by means of a bell. A cell is a lonely place, where a prisoner sits and faces the reality of what he has done; some pray, some cry, and other shout and bawl: but in the end they all want something, and the only way to get it is by ringing that bell.

Witney rang the bell and asked to see Mr Chitty. He had decided to make a more truthful statement, which read as follows:

> 'As God is my judge I had absolutely nothing to do with the shooting of three policemen. I just drove down into Braybrook Street, where a small car pulled up alongside.

Two men got out and one asked if it was my car. I said yes. Then he asked me for my road fund licence, and I told him I didn't have one. The elder of the two policemen walked round to the other side of the car and said, 'Let's have a look in here.' Without anything further Roberts leant across and shot the young officer in the face. The sound of the shot deafened and dazed me. The other officer ran to the front and Roberts, followed by Duddy, gave chase, still shooting. I saw the second officer stumble and fall. Roberts fired again, I don't know how many times. Duddy raced alongside and shot through the window of the police car. They ran back to the car, jumped in, and said 'Drive."

We now had the names of the other two: Roberts and Duddy.

The flat in Maida Vale where Roberts had been living was searched. Mrs Colin Howard and her two children were found to be living there as well as a Mrs Lillian Perry. Lillian Perry was interviewed at length, and she confirmed that she had been with Roberts over the weekend of the shootings. They had stayed in the Russell Hotel in London's Russell Square. On the Monday morning Roberts had bought camping gear, a rucksack and tinned food, and they went to the Wake Arms public house in Epping Forest, where they split up. Shortly after this we received another REGROUP message to go to the Wake Arms.

A plan was put into place, and for days we searched the forest. We found everything from stolen cars, false number plates, perverts' collections, and a full-size crucifix, but nothing to relate to Harry Roberts.

While we were having a tea break we heard an announcement on a transistor radio that Duddy had been arrested in Glasgow. We all cheered at the news!

Joe Public thinks that when a police operation is being carried out every officer in the force knows all that is going on. This is far from the truth. That evening I telephoned my uncle, Davy Morris, a Detective in the City of Glasgow Police Force, for the inside story.

'So you got Duddy then?' I said.

'Oh aye, nae trouble to the Glasgow Polis. If you want a hand down there, we'll come down and help you out.'

Of course, he was only joking. The whole of the country's constabulary was united in getting these killers. Kill a cop and the rest are after you!

'Aye,' Davy said, 'the CID gaffer, Detective Chief Inspector Bob Brown, knew Duddy's family, including his brother, Charles. Charles set his brother up. He went with the police to a tenement in Stephenson Street. At the front door Charlie shouted "It's me, Charlie", and with that the police burst in. Your man was more frightened of the polis than the guns they were carrying. He's coming down to you tonight.'

For the next few weeks we continued to get calls that Roberts had been seen at a million-and-one-different locations.

The trial of the two arrested men was set for Monday, 15th November, 1966.

On Sunday the 14th, at about midnight, I returned to the Lea Bridge Road Section House. In my 'pigeonhole' was a note: 'Parade in uniform - Leytonstone 3 a.m.'

I snatched a few hours sleep and then, with other members of the SPG Unit, went for a briefing at Leytonstone Police Station. Inspector Les David, the inspector in charge of Three Unit SPG, gave the briefing.

A hideout had been found near Bishop's Stortford in Hertfordshire. Roberts' prints had been found inside, and we were to search an area called Thorley Wood. After a five minute briefing the Guv'nor gave us his final words:

'We will head out of here now, no blues, and most of all no sirens. On our way up there I want you to keep your eyes open for a café; we require refreshments.'

Typical of the Guv'nor; he looked after his men on all operations. Perhaps this came from his wartime service in submarines.

We found a café, and much to the dismay of the long-distance lorry drivers we pulled in to the car park. They were under the impression it was some form of raid. The sense of relief could be felt as we ordered some forty bacon-and-egg sandwiches and the same amount of teas.

We arrived in total darkness, parked our vehicles and climbed over a dry stone wall and waited for dawn. Some Flying Squad officers were with us, but most of the search party was made up of the SPG and Hertfordshire officers.

On a given signal we formed a line and walked across the ploughed field. Some of the Hertfordshire officers were carrying .303 Enfield rifles. In a wooded area we came across some underground bunkers, and I lifted the heavy metal lid and climbed in. With a seek-and-search searchlight I could see that the concrete floors were covered with inches of filthy water. It was obvious no one had been in the place for years.

A BBC film crew had been filming the incident for *Panorama*. As they drove away a farmer beckoned me over. 'While you were searching down there a guy with a red beard was behind a wall over there. He ran into that barn.' He pointed to a Dutch barn.

Two Hertfordshire officers came up to me, their .303 rifles slung over their shoulders, and I relayed the information.

'That's OK, Jock, we'll have a look,' one said.

After a couple of minutes I started walking towards the barn and I saw three men coming in my direction - the two officers and the bearded man. As I reached them, they were putting the man with the red beard into the back of the farmer's Land Rover. He was handcuffed by now, and I reached over and searched him. He was not carrying any firearms.

He looked at me and I said, 'Are you Harry Roberts?'

'So fucking what?' he replied.

I got on my radio. 'Urgent message for Uniform One from Uniform 561.'

'Uniform One to Uniform 561, go ahead,' David Powis replied.

'Uniform 561 to Uniform One, Harry Roberts has been arrested and is in the Land Rover heading towards you.'

It was perhaps the most satisfying radio message I ever sent.

On Monday, 15th November, 1966, Duddy and Witney appeared at Number One Court of the Old Bailey, the Central Criminal Court. They were indicted on ten counts. They pleaded Not Guilty to all of them.

Sir Elwyn Jones QC, the Attorney General, opened the case for the Crown in front of Mr Justice Glyn-Jones. The jury was made up of nine men and three women. This was the first time the story of what happened on that horrific day of 12th August, 1966 in Braybrook Street was made public.

The proceedings were interrupted and the court was then told that Roberts had been arrested. The trial was adjourned until 6th December, when Roberts pleaded Guilty to the murder of Detective Sergeant Head and Detective Constable Wombwell. After the judge had finished his summing up, the jury took only thirty minutes to return Guilty verdicts against all three men for the murder of the three policemen.

When passing sentence, Mr Justice Glyn-Jones said,

> 'I pass upon you the sentence prescribed by law for the crime of murder, on each count of which you have been convicted, that is to say imprisonment for life. You have been justly convicted of what is perhaps the most heinous crime to have been committed in this country for a generation or more. I think it likely that no Home Secretary, regarding the enormity of your crime, will ever think fit to show mercy by releasing you on licence. This is one of those cases in which the sentence of imprisonment for life may well be treated as meaning exactly what it says. Lest any Home Secretary in the future should be minded to consider your release on licence, I have to make a recommendation. My recommendation is that you should not be released on licence, any of the three of you, for a period of thirty years to begin from today's date.'

I continued to be interested in the Shepherd's Bush killings, as they became known. Apart from the gravity of the offences, I had the interest of having been in at the arrest, together with my uncle's connection with Duddy in Glasgow.

When I was eventually posted to C11, the Criminal Intelligence Unit, I had access to the Criminal Records Bureau at New Scotland Yard. On a number of occasions I would draw Roberts' file and read about his convictions and background.

He had numerous convictions. These were as follows:

Essex County Quarter Sessions. 21 months for breaking - aged fifteen. In 1954, at the Central Criminal Court, he was convicted for assault with intent to rob. Roberts had cut an old man's finger off while trying to steal a ring. He was sentenced to seven years' imprisonment. On this occasion, Roberts had appeared in front of Mr Justice Maude, who stated: 'You. acting together with another man, brought death pretty near to this old man. You, yourself, have come close to the rope. You don't seem to know that the maximum sentence for robbery with violence is life imprisonment. You are a brutal man.' The other man was acquitted. Roberts was then twenty-one.

This was as far as my interest went; after all Roberts was 'banged up' and would not be released for a long time, despite his claims to other prisoners that he would escape.

After *Undaunted* was first published I kept hearing various stories about the antics of Roberts whilst he was in prison. Apparently, when serving time he was working in the prison kitchen and his 'party piece' was making cakes shaped like gingerbread men. The difference with Roberts' efforts was that they had daggers sticking into them, with red dye running from the figures. He also produced 'artworks' of someone shooting a police officer. These were precisely drawn and coloured.

In 2009 he was allowed day release and celebrated with a champagne party held in a bowling alley. Roberts was returned to prison when it was discovered that whilst on licence he was working at St Bernard's Animal Sanctuary in Derbyshire, which was run by a family who helped the community by taking on former criminals as farm workers. They had no idea one of their workers was the notorious killer Harry Roberts. However, they were soon to learn the truth, after they were subjected to threats from him. These coincided with attacks on the animals. A horse's head was attacked with an axe on the day the family was due to give evidence to the Parole Board. It was as a result of this he was returned to a closed prison in 2010.

He remained in prison until November 2014, when the Parole Board for England and Wales approved his release. This despite the then Home Secretary Theresa May saying at the Police Federation Conference in September 2013 that under the Conservatives those convicted of killing a police officer will have their sentences raised to the 'whole life' category, usually reserved for the very worst types of murder.

On Friday, 12th August, 2016 I attended a memorial service

at Braybrook Street in Shepherd's Bush to remember the three police officers killed fifty years before. At the exact time the killings had taken place a group of about 250 people present stood in silence as a mark of respect. All our thoughts went back fifty years, as if it was yesterday

Grandchildren of the murdered officers laid wreaths at the memorial to the three policemen; grandchildren and the extended family whose lives had been changed forever by the actions of Roberts and his murdering team.

And what about Roberts?

He signs autographs for anyone who is sick enough to buy one. The cost is ONE HUNDRED POUNDS.

Whilst in prison Roberts described his actions on that day as 'Five seconds of madness that changed my life.'

No, it wasn't. It was a life of badness that changed hundreds of innocent people's lives forever.

NINE

AN EXTENDED BEAT

Life went back to normal in the SPG. We were travelling all over the Metropolitan Police District, and literally did not know where the next day would take us. On Sunday, 16th March, 1969 I was about to eat my Sunday lunch when the phone rang. It was Dick Pearce from the SPG. Dick had a habit of blowing down his nose like a boxer in a championship fight.

'Jock, Dick here. Sniff, sniff.'

'Yes, Dick, what's going on?'

'I'm up at the Yard. I've got to ask you three questions.'

'Is this a wind up?'

'Sniff. It's deadly serious.'

'Go on.'

'Do you suffer from sea sickness?'

'No.'

'Do you suffer from air sickness? Sniff, sniff.'

'No.'

'Are you prepared to be away from home for three months?'

Curiosity was now kicking in.

'Yes.'

'Be at the Yard tomorrow at 9.00am.'

'What's it all about?'

'Can't say, sniff. Oh! Be in plainclothes, sniff.'

The next morning we met up at the Yard and were ushered

into the Conference Room. We all stood up as an Assistant Commissioner walked in, followed by other high-ranking officers and military officers, none of whom we had seen before.

The Assistant Commissioner introduced himself and the other officers. We sat in silence as he told us we were going to be flown to the Caribbean to reinstate law and order to Anguilla, a small island - 35 square miles, population 6,080 - where one of the locals, Ronald Webster, had declared its independence. We would assist Number Two Parachute Regiment, who would help take control of the island.

The officer in charge of 2nd Para was a young Acting Captain, Mike Jackson, who was later to become General Sir Mike Jackson. He retired in 2006 as Chief of the General Staff of the British Army.

'Gentlemen,' he said, 'you will leave here and you will be briefed on the operation. Do not discuss this matter outside this room. You will be AN EXTENDED BEAT away from home for about three months. Will this cause anyone any difficulty?'

Silence. Then one hand was raised.

'Yes?' The Assistant Commissioner looked up into the assembled men.

'It's only a small thing, Sir, but it will cause my wife and neighbours a problem. I am having some crazy paving delivered and it will be dropped off in front of my house. I will not have time to put it into the rear garden.

A sigh went round the room. The officers looked at each other. Here we are going across the world to take back an island and he's worried about his crazy paving.

An inspector looked up. 'Leave it with me, we will get some recruits from the Training School to move it.'

'Thank you, Sir, much appreciated.'

We filed out of the room and made our way to the canteen. As we sat down to our breakfast, the 'crazy paving' officer arrived. 'Sorry about that, I had to make a phone call. I had some broken paving to order from the local Council.'

We looked up in disbelief. 'What? You've just ordered it?'

'Well, you didn't expect me to carry that load through to my rear garden?!'

He looked at us and smiled. Now that's what I call initiative!

The next 24 hours were hectic, getting kit ready and sorting things out at home.

By the middle of the week we were circling Anguilla in a military aircraft, the rear door open and a load of paratroopers, dripping with all the accoutrements of war, ready to jump into action. We sat in lightweight Met Police uniforms scrounged from the stores at Brixton and our truncheons.

The Para's 'jump master' stood at the open rear door, his outstretched right arm holding on to a handle, his other hand pressed against his headphones. He looked back into the aircraft, held up his left hand and raised his thumb. The Paras stood up and connected their static lines to an overhead cable, and started to shuffle down towards the rear door. The engines droned as the aircraft banked and flew across the island. I remember being amazed how blue and clear the sea was. I had never been out of the UK before.

The jump master pressed his hand against his headphones again and then looked round at the men, and with a look of disappointment shouted something into the ear of the soldier next to him. The word was passed down the line. One by one the look of disappointment appeared on each face as they received the message: 'No resistance, landing strip secured.'

The aircraft landed and when we disembarked we were greeted by what seemed to be the whole of Fleet Street. We commandeered the local school for our billet; our bed was the concrete floor. We then had to commandeer some vehicles until ours arrived from the UK, and a few of us went out with some soldiers and set up a roadblock. The Paras took over laying rocks along the road to slow down any approaching cars. They then mounted machine guns on either side of the ditches.

'OK, when you see a vehicle you fancy, step out and stop it. We will keep you covered,' one Para said.

A mini mope being driven by an elderly man pulled up. We got out our piece of paper issued to us and started to read it to him. 'By the powers invested in me by Her Majesty Queen Elizabeth...'

We got no further. Two women were walking towards the soldiers, each carrying kitchen chairs.

'You boys don't want to be lying here gettin' yerselves all dirty and getting burnt by de sun. Now you go and sit in di shade and I'll get some water.'

The Paras climbed out of the ditch, dusting themselves down and shaking their heads as they made themselves comfortable in the chairs while the woman poured them some ice-cold water.

Meanwhile, we were trying to tell our driver that we were going to take his car. It looked like trouble was brewing until we told him how much the British Government was going to pay him.

'No trouble man, I take you to ma cousin's, dae got good cars for dae same money.'

We all burst out laughing as our new-found car hire tycoon slapped our backs. So ended our roadblocks!

We soon settled in and got on with patrols around the island, and met up with a SAS team who had parachuted on to the island prior to our arrival. Two Special Branch officers, Mike Waller and Harry Gardner, were also there. Mike later became Margaret Thatcher's bodyguard.

The SAS team had done a magnificent job in finding weapons hidden at various locations. SPG officers went to these locations and took possession of the weapons, many of which were old and in poor condition.

We had a few riots stirred up by the usual bunch of troublemakers that can be found anywhere in the world. These were soon brought under control.

While on patrol one evening, accompanied by our usual complement of soldiers, we heard noises coming from a corrugated shack. We crept up and looked through a slit in the wall. Inside were some men lounging about drinking. We opened the door and walked in, much to the surprise of the occupants. They made us very welcome and told stories of 'Her Majesty Queen Elizabeth'. They were so proud of having 'met their Queen', albeit standing in a crowd as she passed by!

They had been threatened by Ronald Webster that they would have big voodoo trouble if they spoke about the Queen. After a few more beers one of the men left, returning a short time later carrying an old rusty biscuit tin. He opened the lid, reached in and removed the Union Flag, together with a framed picture of the Queen. He walked over to some nails sticking out of the wall and hung both of them back in their rightful place. We stood to attention as they got up from their chairs and sang the National Anthem. They sang every verse, while we mumbled through the last few. We felt proud to have witnessed the loyalty of these people, so far from our shores.

Over the next few weeks we managed to get the island back to some form of normality. Winston, a prisoner on bail for murder using a knife, continued to cut our hair with an open razor!

Eventually, we returned to England strapped into webbing seats in the hold of a Hercules aircraft. I took a week's leave in Scotland with my wife, Janet. It had been our first wedding anniversary while I was in Anguilla, a fact I've never been allowed to forget.

While I was in Scotland I received a telephone call from Detective Inspector Trevor Lloyd-Hughes.

'Jim, C11 (the Criminal Intelligence Department at New Scotland Yard) are looking for a photographer to work undercover; it's right up your street. You've got an interview with Commander Hoggins in two days' time.'

We drove straight back to London and I had the interview with Mr Norman Hoggins, one of life's true gentlemen. I was accepted. In some ways I was sorry to be leaving the Group. They were a good bunch of guys with a truly great guv, Inspector Leslie David. However, a posting to Scotland Yard had been a boyhood ambition and I looked to the future with unclouded optimism.

TEN

MONDAY MORNING AND A NEW LIFE

Made it! I had been accepted for the Criminal Intelligence Department. After six years in the job and hundreds of arrests, I had reached Scotland Yard. This, I believed, would give me the opportunity to catch some 'real' villains.

Monday morning, off of the tube at St James' and a short walk across the road to New Scotland Yard. In I went through the revolving doors, past the glass case with the eternal flame flickering and the book of remembrance lying open naming the officers who had been killed on duty. The pages were turned daily. That day it was in memory of the officers killed in Foxtrot 11.

I showed my warrant card, walked past the reception desk and into the lift and up to the fourth floor. I turned left and walked along the corridor past the identical bland doors with small business-card signs naming the various offices fixed to the aluminium frames.

Eventually I found 'CO C11 Criminal Intelligence'. The door was open, and with some trepidation I walked into the office. It was empty apart from one officer answering the phones. He looked up at me and signalled 'one minute'. I stood at the counter. I looked to my left along the office, which appeared to be never-ending, with rows of desks set out in T-formation. The detective inspector's 'carver-type' chair was at the head of the T. Each desk had wooden filing-trays filled with folders. Hanging from the ceiling above the appropriate desks were the district signs, one to four, marking out the then four districts of the Metropolitan Police. One Imperial typewriter, issued to each district, sat on the desks.

Nearer the door were rows of filing cabinets.

The officer put the phone down.

'Can I help you?'

'Yes, I'm Jim Smith, I've come to join C11 today.'

'What district?'

'Photographic.'

'Go and have a cup of tea in the canteen, he won't be here until at least 10 o'clock, Jock.'

I looked at my watch, it was only 8.30am. I walked round the corner to the canteen and sat down with my tea. The place was empty apart from the occasional uniform officers coming in to collect trays of teas. I leafed through a copy of *The Job*, the Met Police's own newspaper.

'Good morning, what brings you up here at this time?'

I looked up. It was Detective Sergeant John Groves, my next door neighbour; the man who would hardly speak to me when I was in uniform. Had he suddenly had a brain transplant?

'Oh, good morning, I'm just waiting for some staff to arrive, I'm joining C11 today.'

'Oh, they'll arrive eventually. It's a different ball game up here.'

Never a truer word was spoken, as I was to find out over the next few years. He then strode off, shoulders high with his distinctly arrogant swagger.

Time passed slowly, and eventually a DC walked over to me. He was dressed in a pin-striped suit with highly-polished brogue shoes. He looked as if he had just stepped out the window of Gieves and Hawkes on Savile Row.

'DC Smith?'

'Yes.'

'I'm John, the Guv'nor will see you now.'

As I followed him to the office, I thought he might be the Guv'nor's butler.

I entered the C11 office and was introduced to Detective Chief Inspector 'Nosher' Powell. His blond Brylcreemed hair was brushed back and his arms were folded across his chest as he studied some architect's drawings of a yacht spread out on his desk.

He looked up and turned round.

'Good morning, you must be TDC Smith.'

'Yes, Sir.'

'Good morning, welcome to C11. What do you know about us?'

'Not very much, Sir, other than no-one seems to talk about what goes on up here.'

'Good that's the way we like it. We target top criminals by various means.'

I nodded.

'Do you know anything about the 'various means'?'

'I've heard about phone taps, but don't know anything about the system other than a bit about the photographic side.'

'Good, the intercept side won't affect you other than going to cover 'meets'. You will soon settle in. It seems a bit strange when you come here at first. I'm sure you'll blend in OK... You like my boat?' he asked, as he saw me looking at the drawings.

I'm thinking to myself, this guy likes a joke. This boat's worth a small fortune.

'What, is it involved in a job, Sir?'

'No, no, it's mine. I'm having it built in Holland and when I retire I will cruise round the world on it.'

He's diverting me. It's a big job he's involved with!

'My old aunt died and left me some money. I've invested it in the boat, God bless her!'

This was a long way from 'knickers and meat' at the SPG!

'OK then, Jock - you don't mind if I call you, Jock, do you? Let's take you round the office.'

We walked out of his office and I was introduced to various officers.

'This one here is the most important, he approves your expenses.' A rotund detective sergeant looked up, nodded and continued to write in the mountain of diaries in front of him. He picked up a new diary and handed it to me.

in its place. The villains had a black-and-fawn coloured Austin Princess and a dark blue Ford Transit Van. There was no doubt they had inside information. Using the Princess they rammed the Consul head-on, severely injuring the BSA staff inside. The gang, using axes and baseball bats, then smashed their way into the car. A guard was dragged out and the cash box, which was chained to his arm, was cut off using heavy-duty boltcutters. Inside the box was £41,000.

The robbers piled into the Transit and made off with the cash.

Later that day, waiting in their vehicles in Barry Road, East Dulwich, London, was a Flying Squad team. The team consisted of DI Mathews, DS Stanley Chrichton, DS Henry Robertson, DC David Dixon and Detective Sergeant 'Little Legs' Frank Lovejoy. The time was approximately 10.15pm. The robbers were arrested when they returned to the house at No 48; a total of £29,334 was recovered from the house. Almost £12,000 was missing.

The day after the robbery one of the robbers, Michael David Kehoe, who had been arrested and taken to Steelhouse Lane Police Station in Birmingham, was questioned by Detective Cecil Lewis about the missing money. His answer was, 'If I told you who had it, you still wouldn't get it back, so there isn't much point, but what I will tell you is it went to connections in Birmingham.'

On 5th January, 1966, DCI Reginald Scragg questioned Anthony Lucraft at Ilford Police Station. Mr Scragg informed Lucraft that a Birmingham newspaper dated 14th December, 1965, had been found in the house at Barry Road, and on that paper they had found Lucraft's fingerprints. Lucraft was charged in connection with the robbery. On 20th January, 1966, at the Central lock-up in Birmingham, Detective Sergeant Light saw Lucraft, at the prisoner's request. The conversation went as follows:

'I understand you want to see me?'

He was cautioned.

'Yes, but I want to tell you what my connection is with this robbery. I've always said that I didn't take part in it. What happened was Kehoe came to my house after he had done it, and asked me to count the money. I gave him some paper bags to put it in. I am surprised you didn't find my fingerprints all over the money.'

Lucraft denied having any of the proceeds of the crime. Kehoe, Thwaites, Ware and Lewis were each sentenced to twelve years' imprisonment. Anthony Lucraft was found guilty and was sentenced to four years' imprisonment.

So, where did the £12,000 go?

Some twenty years later I was working with a former Flying Squad officer, who has since passed away. He told me where it went!

ELEVEN

THE GUN RUNNER

During 1970 a Flying Squad Officer came in to see me at the C11 office.

'Jock, I need your services this afternoon.'

'It will cost you.'

'Typical Sweaty comment.'

'Go on, what is it?'

'Come round to the canteen and I'll buy you a coffee.'

We sat down in the coffee shop, and in a whispered conversation he began.

'I've got a snout that has come up with some very good info. All his past info has been spot on. He's been approached by a geezer who wants to buy some rifles.'

'A Paddy?'

'No, he's a 'bubble' (Bubble and squeak: Greek) or something similar. He wants to buy a load. My man says it's enough to supply a small army. We haven't a clue whether it is IRA or any others. You Jocks are not rising up against us are you? Anyway, I've been put in touch with the guy and I'm going in to meet him as a dealer. I'm seeing him this afternoon at the Cumberland Hotel, in the Nocturne Bar at 3.00pm. I've arranged to pick up a brand new SLR from Wellington Barracks to show him as a sample. In case you don't know, an SLR is a self-loading rifle.'

'Of course I do, I saw service in Anguilla.'

'Oh, I forgot - a war veteran, sorry, sorry. Can you cover the meeting?'

'Yes, I'll be there. Have you got a description?'

'Yes, the geezer has a face like a dried chamois and a handlebar moustache, so even you should be able to pick him out!'

'Yes, I think I can manage that, and what with you walking in with your rifle up over your shoulder, he should pick you out easily enough.'

'No, you tosser, the rifle will be in the back of the squad car.'

'Oh, really?'

'Yeah, yeah - it will be wrapped in waxed brown paper.'

'Yes, OK, I'll be there and get as close to your car as possible.'

'We are using the Rover, I'll get you the registration number we are putting on it.'

At half-past two I climbed into the back of the observation van in the basement of Scotland Yard. My driver took me up into Seymour Street, where we saw the squad Rover parked. We managed to park next to it and I had a good view from the rear of the vehicle. After about five minutes, the squad 'dealer' walked past the doorman into the hotel to meet with the gunrunner.

Twenty minutes later I saw the dealer coming out with a Greek-looking male. The dealer walked to the rear of the Rover and opened the boot. I could clearly see some canvas bags being moved, and the Greek bending over and looking into the boot. He stood up and then shook hands with the dealer. He had a broad smile on his face. He turned to face the hidden camera and the Nikon purred as I ran off 10-20 frames.

After they left my driver returned and we drove back to Scotland Yard. I processed the photos, indexed them and after a few hours I was showing them to the Flying Squad team.

'Oh, well done, Jock, excellent pictures, there's no mistaking him. Thanks, you've done a great job, I wish our tossers had had the same results - they lost him in Cricklewood. We'll try to set up another meet. I'll tell you this, Jim, when he saw the shooter in the back of the car, his eyes came out like a whippet's balls.'

To the best of my knowledge, no further meets were ever kept. Questions were left unanswered. Did he leave the country? Did he die, or had he pulled out of the business?

I had to wait until 1977 to get the answers.

TWELVE

THE FRENCH CONNECTION

The canteen at Scotland Yard was situated on the fourth floor. I was queuing for a coffee when I heard a voice from behind.

'What you doing here, Smith?'

It was John French, a detective I had met some years previously when I had been working at Bow Street Police Station. John had been on the original Kray Squad under the command of Superintendent 'Nipper' Read. He was now posted to C11. From that day on we worked together whenever we could. John had an unequalled knowledge of London criminals, in fact on the day I introduced him to Keith that was how I described John, and Keith's reply was, 'We shall see, we shall see.'

We did see, and it was not long before finally Keith did too.

Whenever we had a spare moment, John would drive the observation van with me hidden in the rear. We would cruise round the West End and the Hatton Garden area, where he would point out top villains to me to photograph; it was like a turkey shoot. In the 'Garden' it was mostly receivers of stolen jewellery he spotted.

While in the Soho area, John saw two men walking down Greek Street.

'Get these two.'

I ran off a few frames, and went back to the Yard and processed the films. I was sitting in my office indexing the films when Commander Dave Dilley walked past.

'What you got there, son?'

'It's two guys John knows'

I shouted down the empty office.

'John, what's the name of these two geezers from Greek Street?'

'Bernie Silver and Big Frank Mifsud.'

Dave Dilley reached over and picked up a couple of my pictures, studied them and then asked to see the rest.

'Who asked you to take them?'

'Nobody, Guv'nor, we were driving through Soho when John spotted them.'

'That's 'Old Bernie'; he's a has-been, yesterday's man, he's finished. We don't want to clutter up the system with people like them. Give me all the pictures and the negatives and I'll dump them for you.'

With that he took all of the pictures and the negatives.

'Is this job recorded any place?' Dilley asked.

'No, I was just about to put it in the book when you arrived.'

'That's fine, don't bother putting any entry in the book. Keep up the good work. Well done mate.'

Bernie Silver and Frank Mifsud were the biggest pornographers in the country. No photographs of them existed in the C11 Indices. Silver was responsible for corrupting some officers at West End Central Police Station. The very station where Dilley served as Detective Sergeant.

Wally Virgo, as Commander in charge of C1, was in overall charge of all the CID including the Murder Squad and the 'Porn' Squad (Obscene Publication Squad). The officer in charge of this squad was Bill Moody. Mr Virgo had a particular interest in this department; then, of course, he would have. It was revealed at his subsequent trial that he was on the payroll of the vice syndicate running Soho. He was 'earning' £1,500 per week from them. Both he and Moody, along with a number of other officers, were jailed for periods of up to eight years. I find it very difficult to believe that the head of the Criminal Intelligence Department was not aware of what was going on.

Some time later, CID officers were arrested for corruption. They were filmed and tape recorded as they tried to plant evidence on a

South London 'toe rag'. *The Times* published the story and these officers became known as 'the firm within a firm'.

Dilley was furious, and called me into his office. He had come up with the bright idea of having me photograph every photographer and reporter in Fleet Street. Three days later he realized the enormity of the task and cancelled it.

As a favour, I had once driven a fresh-faced Detective Constable to his building society where he collected £200 from his account. He sat in the van next to me counting the money, which he then put into an 'On Her Majesty's Service' envelope.

'That's too much for me, I was only giving you a lift. You would have done better getting a taxi,' I said.

'Piss off, you prat, it's for DD. I've got my sergeant's board tomorrow and Dilley is sitting on my selection board. This will ensure I get through. He likes a "drink"' when he sits on any selection board.'

It worked - DD took the money, and yet another young officer was being 'groomed' in the corrupt ways of some of the higher echelons in the CID. The officer passed the selection board, no doubt assisted by DD's 'drink'. He continued to climb the ladder to a very senior position within the Metropolitan Police.

The next time I met him was some years later at the Old Bailey.

'Hi, Jim, how are things going?' I asked.

He looked at me as if I was a bit of dog muck stuck to his shoe, and with his nose in the air he walked past. Why? Did he think I was going to remind him of how he got through his sergeant's CID board? Or, did he think I was going to tell Her Majesty what her envelopes were being used for?

In May 1972 Sir Robert Mark called a meeting of all senior CID officers and read the riot act to them. Shortly afterwards, all C11 units received radio messages telling them to return to the office at once. We returned believing a major operation was about to take place. We could not have been more wrong; it was for a pep talk from none other than Dave Dilley. The office was crowded. He stood on a chair, reminiscent of former Commissioner Sir John Nott-Bower, who, in 1955, had stood on a chair in West End Central Police Station to address CID officers and tell them he did not believe Superintendent Bert Hannam's report that had said there was corruption in the police and in the West End Central in particular.

Dilley's speech started by telling everyone that he, along with other senior members of the CID, had been to see the new Commissioner, who had told them in no uncertain manner that they represented what had long been the most routinely corrupt organization in London, and that nothing or no-one would prevent him putting an end to it, and if necessary he would put the whole of the CID back into uniform and make a fresh start.

I can to this day remember his main line: 'The good times are over. There is no longer any chance of 'doing business'. If you have got anything going, get out of it now.'

The address lasted about ten minutes and then we all dispersed, all except one officer who went into Dilley's office and closed the door. After a few minutes, he came out wandered over to me.

'What was that all about?' I asked.

'The hypocritical old rascal, I've just been in his office and bunged him £400 from a job we had off.'

THIRTEEN

LUNCH WITH THE
DUKE OF EDINBURGH

In 1973 Detective Chief Inspector John Groves was appointed to C11. He was responsible for all operations. The first operation that I recall was when he entered the office in company with Dave Dilley. Groves pointed at 'specially chosen officers', myself included. There were about ten of us chosen, we gathered round the two senior officers and listened as Groves addressed us.

'Be in the office at 12.00 noon, we have an operation commencing at 1.00pm in Portman Square.'

As usual with any type of operation when we had not been told any details, there was a lot of guessing as to what it might be, although we could never have guessed this one.

12.00 noon arrived and once again we gathered round Groves and Dilley. Groves spoke as Dilley stood silent next to him, a smile on his face.

'Gentlemen, we are going to the Churchill Hotel for lunch with the Grand Order of Water Rats. It will be attended by the Duke of Edinburgh and numerous personalities. A number of guests have been unable to attend, and rather than have an empty table the Duke's protection officer has asked us to make up the numbers.'

I found this tale hard to believe. Specially chosen officers? What a load of rubbish, the only reason we were chosen was on that day we were wearing suits! To be perfectly honest, none of us gave it a second thought; it was a free lunch with Tommy Cooper doing the cabaret.

It was only a few years later when some of the facts came out.

At the time, the Churchill Hotel was owned by the Loews US Corporation, and an Eric Miller was the developer. Miller, a Jewish boy, had been brought up in St John's Wood in London. At the age of sixteen, when he was working in an estate agents, his talent for the trade was spotted by George Farrow, who ran a small company called Peachey. Farrow headhunted Miller. Some time later, Farrow died and Miller became the chairman of Peachey. The company expanded into the commercial property market.

Things did not go as well as expected and Miller got involved with a former Rachman solicitor and casino entrepreneur by the name of Judah Binstock, a master fraudsman. His activities at this time were being investigated by Detective Sergeant Michael Franklin of C11. Franklin was the sole officer responsible for investigations into casinos, and in particular the Victoria Sporting Club, one of Binstock's interests.

In 1972, Franklin left the Police and joined - yes, you've got it - Judah Binstock's company. Franklin was the sergeant who was responsible for checking our diaries and expenses to make sure everything was correct.

Miller and Binstock became partners in business. Groves and Miller became 'buddies'. Groves took Miller to C11 social functions, which were also attended by none other than David Dilley. The friendship blossomed, with Groves attending 10 Downing Street with Miller as guests of the then Prime Minister, Harold Wilson. Miller, who, on paper at least, was a multi-millionaire, and like his father before him (his father was a Labour Party Councillor) supported the Labour Party, some say financially. In whatever way Eric Miller supported them, it resulted in him receiving a knighthood in Wilson's retirement Honours list in 1976.

Things were not going too well at Peachey's and Sir Eric's thieving was beginning to surface. In an attempt to get out of financial trouble, he demanded £300K from Binstock, which he alleged was owed to him. However, Binstock 'had it on his toes', but not before he was stopped by Customs at Heathrow Airport, on 15th September, 1976. In his briefcase were a number of documents which, when questioned about, he made out to be old and shouldn't have been with him. He then set about tearing them up and threw them in a dustbin. Not the cleverest thing to do, as after his departure to Paris the diligent Customs Officer retrieved the documents from the bin and, with a roll of Sellotape, pieced them together. The documents revealed a multi-million fraud by Binstock and his associates, some of whom were eventually convicted on this evidence. Despite a warrant being issued for Binstock's arrest, it was never executed and he never returned to the UK. He carried on in 'business' in Spain.

Copies of the reassembled documents made their way to various Government bodies including the Treasury, Fraud Squad and the FBI. A bundle arrived in C11, only to be copied by Groves who then took them straight to his mate Miller. Miller was, to say the least, delighted with the information, because he had unsuccessfully hoped to recover the £300K from Binstock and now this evidence would bring down the wrath of the law.

After some time Sir Eric was forced out of Peachey. He was served with four writs for restitution of the funds he had taken and he too awaited the force of the law.

In January 1977 Groves was promoted to Detective Chief Superintendent and posted to H Division, my old stomping ground. Things carried on as normal between the two men, with Sir Eric desperate to find the whereabouts of his old buddy, Judah. However, with Miller facing imprisonment, he committed suicide on 22nd September, 1977 - the Jewish Day of Atonement.

It was not until later, when an article appeared in *Private Eye*, that the excreta hit the fan. Groves had gone to Sir Eric's son's all-expenses-paid Bar Mitzvah 'bash' in Israel, plus receiving loads of other freebies, courtesy of Sir Eric!

John Groves was interviewed and immediately resigned from the Police. On Friday, 5th October, 1979, he was convicted at the Old Bailey for giving the documents to Sir Eric Miller, contrary to the Official Secrets Act. He was cleared of four charges of corruption. Dilley gave evidence at the trial and stated that if he had known about reports by the Fraud Squad naming Miller as a 'very unpleasant person who would screw anyone for a fast buck', he would not have let Groves go to the Bar Mitzvah.

Give me a break! The head of the Criminal Intelligence Department didn't know? At the time, Dilley was still wining and dining at the Churchill Hotel, courtesy of the 'Sir'. He attended yet more Water Rats lunches with him, and it was Miller who 'put in a word for him' which secured him the position of head of security of Sears Holdings on his retirement in August 1976, after being awarded the Queen's Police Medal two weeks before.

Every year C11 had a stag night; it was either held at The Lords Tavern or the Oval cricket grounds. Guests were invited, and the cabaret was usually supplied by top comedians or singers, who 'sang for their supper'. A couple of strippers would appear and perform their 'classic' act.

On one such occasion I could not believe my eyes. Sitting at the head of the top table, between Dilley and 'Wilf' Pickles (the head of the telephone intercept department), was none other than the 'Old Has Been', the pornographer Bernie Silver. Was this another person the head of the Criminal Intelligence was not aware of what he was doing?

Commander Ken Drury's lifestyle changed dramatically when a Sunday newspaper published a story, along with photographs, of 'Big Ken' on an all-expenses paid holiday in Cyprus with another pornographer.

Detective Chief Superintendent Bert Wickstead, 'The Old Grey Fox', formed a squad to investigate the Syndicate. It transpired that the Syndicate had been in existence for eighteen years, and at the later end of their existence were earning an amazing one million pounds per month! The laundering of their funds was so vast that an expert from the Fraud Squad had to be seconded to the investigating squad. This officer was Detective Inspector Bernard Tighe, known throughout the Met as BT, and was a leading figure in the arrest and conviction of the pornographers Bernie Silver and Frank Mifsud.

I first worked with BT when he was attending the funeral of a London criminal. An informant had agreed to point out a criminal who was involved in some form of international fraud. It was thought that the suspect would return from abroad to pay his respects. I was hidden some 200 yards from the crematorium steps, viewing proceedings through a 400mm lens. BT arrived with the informant, an elderly Jewish gentleman. Both were wearing skullcaps. I was running off rolls of film as I photographed the mourners arriving and making their way into the service.

After about half an hour, the service finished and the mourners spilled out. BT, 'a good Catholic boy', appeared to have gone through a conversion. He was now 'a good Jewish boy', with his outstretched hands - palms upwards and his head shrunk into his shoulders - emphasizing every word spluttering out of his mouth. This was an Oscar-winning performance! It had to be photographed.

In the office at C11 was a noticeboard where unknown associates of criminals were displayed for identification purposes. BT's picture was displayed on the board for suggestions as to the identity of the subject. MANY names were suggested!

On leaving the police BT entered the private sector, where I have had the pleasure to work with him up to the present time. We have had many successful operations saving revenue for international companies worldwide.

FOURTEEN
FINGERED!

During the mid-1960s a group of Australian criminals came to Britain, where they were to ply their trade for almost a decade. The composition of the group was ever-changing; sometimes there could be as many as twenty operating at any given time. They were 'likeable rogues', who never used violence and specialised in shoplifting - not a Mars Bar out of Woolworths, mind you, more likely a £100,000 necklace from Garrard, the Crown jewellers. They specialized in a con called 'diversion theft'.

One morning, a team of about a half-dozen of them entered Barclays Bank at Piccadilly. Some joined the queue, while others occupied themselves by filling out paying-in slips. As members of the team reached the head of the queue, others interrupted the counter staff. 'Excuse me love, can I use your toilet? I'm bustin' for a piss,' one asked.

'We don't have public toilets, Sir.'

'Where do you piss, my lovely?'

With that, his teammates joined in verbally to create a little chaos.

'Get the manager, he's drunk,' they shouted.

Then another would approach the 'drunk' and start shouting at him.

'Sorry, sorry, I've got a medical condition,' the lead actor would protest.

While this commotion was going on, two of the gang were using telescopic transistor-radio aerials with hooks on the end to pull travellers cheques from behind the screens. At this stage, the 'drunk' started to urinate against the wall of the bank. The two 'good citizens' then took him by the arms and ejected from him from the bank, while the others vanished into Piccadilly with unsigned travellers cheques to the value of £90,000. By the close of business that day, £30,000 of these had been cashed in Scotland!

It became known that the gang was using a watering hole in Bayswater called the Dennis Club. Jim Clarke, a detective from C11, and I kept observation on the club every Sunday morning for months. I had photographed most of the gang by the end of the operation. Unbeknownst to them, they had greatly assisted me by taking turns to sit at the open windows.

We were aware that corrupt police officers were being paid by these Aussies. Rumours were going around that when they were working, each carried £1,000 pounds to pay off any arresting officer, should they be caught. A secret operation was put in place by Detective Inspector Dave Woodland. All the photographs I had taken were kept at my home. The photographs were put into albums by myself, my wife and my father-in-law, Lt Colonel William Murray of the Salvation Army, for use in relation to any forthcoming job they pulled. It was Dave Woodland's intention to 'nick as many Aussies as possible and put the cat amongst the pigeons' while Dilley was on holiday.

On 6th April, 1972, the albums were issued to selected officers. Dave Woodland and other officers travelled to Manchester, as he had information that the Aussies were going to travel up country to carry out some robberies 'in the sticks'.

The following day, WDC Haylett and I boarded the 7.45am train to Manchester at Euston Station. On the train were a group of Aussies going to work. When the train stopped at Wimslow, I got into the carriage with the Aussies. It was surreal; the people sitting opposite did not know the new passenger sitting facing them, yet I knew every line and mole on their faces, having been up close to them for months with a very powerful telephoto lens.

At Manchester, they got off the train and split up, but

remaining within thirty feet of each other. Within two hours of their arrival in the city centre they had entered three banks and stolen thousands of pounds worth of blank travellers cheques. They then went to the Automobile Association offices, where they stole unused international driving licences. All the stolen goods were put into pre-prepared envelopes, which were then posted to Australia House in London to be collected by them the following day.

All bar one were arrested on their return to Manchester station, and the stolen property was recovered from the Post Office. The one who escaped capture was a man by the name of William Lloyd, but he was arrested two days later at a house in north London. Not incidentally, William had an identical twin who was not part of the arrested group.

All of the team were remanded in custody. We were over the moon with the arrests. At the very least, it proved to certain senior officers that criminals could be followed outside London and arrested for their crimes.

Not long after, I was standing in the lift on the fourth floor at Scotland Yard when the door started to close, but a foot was pushed in, making the door re-open. It was a Flying Squad officer that I knew by sight.

'Oops, sorry about that, I almost cut you in two,' I said.

'That's okay, Jock, let's go up first.'

With that he pressed the button to take us to the top floor. My immediate reaction was that he had been called urgently to another office.

'I've been trying to get hold of you on your own. You know the Australian guys you fingered on the train?' he asked.

'Yes,' I said.

'Here, have a look at this.'

He produced a passport-sized photograph of one of the Lloyd twins.

'Which one of them is that?' he asked.

'It's one of the Lloyd brothers.'

'Which one?'

'Oh, there is no way you can tell from a picture, they're identical twins,' I said.

Meantime, we went from the top floor to the ground floor and up again. As people entered the lift he stopped talking, resuming only when there was the two of us. He then turned the photograph over. Written on the back was the wording: 'This is a true likeness of William Lloyd', and this was dated 6th April 1972. There was also a rubber stamp mark from a company of solicitors in Sydney, Australia.

'This is his brother, Cecil,' the Flying Squad officer said, 'the lads have had it 'dummied up' in Aussie. You will be shown this picture in court. All you need to do is positively say that the man in the dock is the man in the picture and then that will give him outers and then he will walk. Now, the good news is there is three grand in it for you. They will not let you down, the cash is there waiting for you. Don't worry about me, I've already been weighed in. Are you up for it?'

'I'll give it a bit of thought,' I replied.

'Good man.'

He put his arm round my shoulder and gave me a hug. I felt sick.

There was no one I could go to about the matter, and besides, it would be his word against mine. Who would believe me against the word of a Flying Squad sergeant who was a big mate of Commander Ken Drury, the head of the Squad?

I sat at home and discussed the events with my wife. We were totally at a loss as what to do. We both knew I would not take the money. Was the temptation there? Of course it was, our mortgage was £5,500.

Throughout the next few weeks, the corrupt officer gave his new-found 'friend' a knowing wink every time he saw me.

During February 1973 I was called to give evidence at Manchester Crown Court. After I reached the end of my evidence, the prosecution barrister who had lead me through, finished and with the usual 'Thank you, officer, just wait there', as he sat down.

The defence barrister stood up and said, 'Ah, DC Smith, you are an experienced officer and from what you told the court you have seen the Lloyd brothers on numerous occasions, correct?'

'That's correct, Sir.'

'You travelled on the train between London and Manchester and you are the only officer out of the many who has given evidence who can say that my client was on that train, is that correct?'

'Yes, Sir.'

'I would like you to look at this photograph. May I produce this as exhibit WL1?' The court usher took the exhibit and handed it to me.

'DC Smith, I want you to look at the photograph. Do not turn it over until I say so, thank you.'

I took the photograph and looked at it.

'Is this the man you see standing in front of you today?' he asked.

'It is difficult to say, it looks like him.'

'It looks like him? Let's put it another way. Is that the man you saw on the train?'

'From this picture I can only say it could be. He is an identical twin and I cannot say this was the man on the train,' I said.

'Thank you, Officer, turn the photograph over.'

I turned it over.

'Thank you, Officer, now read what it says on the back.'

'This is a true likeness of William Lloyd,' I read.

'Read the date and also the solicitor's name.'

I read it out.

'So you see, Officer, my client was in Australia having his passport photograph taken the day before you say, you, an expert from Scotland Yard, saw him on the train going to Manchester thousands of miles away. Highly unlikely, no, impossible, Officer, would you agree?'

'Yes, Sir, however…'

'No further questions.'

And with that he sat down.

The prosecution barrister stood up.

'DC Smith, you were about to say something before my learned friend sat down, what was that?'

'William Lloyd has the top of his index finger missing. His identical twin does not. The man on the train was William Lloyd and I identified him because of this.'

The Judge intervened: 'Stand up, and hold up your hands,' he said to Lloyd.

Lloyd stood up and held up his hands.

'Show the jury your hands,' the judge ordered.

Lloyd slowly turned round to face the jury as he held his hands up.

I watched as the jury counted his fingers - all nine and a half!

'No further questions, you may stand down,' the barrister said.

I left the witness box. I could feel the accused's eyes burning a hole in me. It must have been that causing the itch on either side of my nose which I had to scratch with my index and middle finger as I passed him.

They were all found guilty and sentenced to three years' imprisonment. They were not happy with me - I could never understand why not? After all, I had saved them three grand!

As for the bent detective sergeant? He never spoke to me again. Perhaps it was just as well, as a few years later he went into a kitchen shop and bought a knife. He then walked to the boutique where his girlfriend worked. He entered the shop and after an argument with her stabbed her to death. Despite the best efforts of his corrupt solicitor, Michael Relton, who himself was subsequently jailed for laundering millions of pounds from the Brink's-Mat robbery, the officer was sent to prison.

FIFTEEN
WATCHING THE ROBBERS

I really felt that I was achieving something in the fight against crime, working with a lot of mainly dedicated and honest police officers who were quite content to remain detective constables or detective sergeants, as long as they could remain in C11 doing their particular job. They were doing the job they loved. These were the frontline officers who every day put their life in danger.

One example was DC Phil Williams, when he was on an operational job following some bank robbers. When they were outside the bank and in the act of drawing their guns, Phil mounted the pavement on his motorcycle and drove at the nearest armed robber. The robber aimed his sawn-off shotgun at Phil and discharged both barrels into his legs. The robber was knocked to the ground by other officers and arrested. Undeterred, Phil then drove at another robber, who drew a 4.5 magnum pistol and fired three shots, all of which narrowly missed Phil's head. For these actions he was awarded the George Medal.

Six years later, when following yet another robber, he was 'sussed' and subsequently knocked off his motorcycle and driven over three times by the villain in his car.

Other officers, including myself, were spending hours in the rear of observation vans with nothing more to eat than sandwiches. The toilet facilities were a plastic bottle to pee in. There was no luxury of air-conditioning or hand washing facilities. When it was hot you cooked, and when it was cold you froze. None of us were looking for any reward or bonuses for what we were doing.

I believe it was the adrenaline rush in beating these devious and cunning criminals that kept us going.

The photographic section at C11 was formed to obtain up-to-date photographs of active criminals. The Criminal Records Office photographs which had been attached to their files frequently had no resemblance to the person in question. This was due to the fact that the photographs on the file were taken at the time of the subject entering prison, and not when they were discharged. 'Funny faces' were frequently pulled by the criminals, knowing that they would not be identified from these. It is hard to believe today that prisoners were not photographed then at police stations.

I was having the time of my life, getting paid to do my hobby and, most of all, being involved in and living a dream come true. During 1971, I was asked by colleagues in C11 to assist them in an observation they were mounting in the City of London. As usual, the briefing for this type of operation was carried out in a quiet area of the canteen in the Yard.

'We've got a line running on a geezer who's making himself busy at the moment. It would appear that he's getting a team together to do a 'blag'. They are going to meet up down the Garden about 3 o'clock,' said one of the officers.

A well-known bank robber had arranged to meet some colleagues in the Hatton Garden area of London to discuss a 'bit of business'. The name of at least one of the robbers involved was known to us.

I loaded my camera equipment into the van. My driver parked in a side road and started filling in betting slips as part of his cover. The suspect duly arrived in company of one other male. There was a considerable amount of radio chat amongst the surveillance units in the area.

The first message I received informed me to proceed with extreme caution, as the men were 'very sussy and were all eyes'. It was not thought that they were going to commit the robbery at this time, but were doing a dry run.

The next message was that the two men were thought to be in contact with another man on the opposite pavement. Apparently, they had been making hand signals. Events unfolded as follows:

'Central 42, are you receiving?'

'Central 42, go ahead over…'

'Central 42, they are walking down towards the *Daily Mirror* building, are you in the vicinity, over?'

'Central 42, I am outside the Evening Standard building, over.'

'Central 42, standby, they have just met up with the third man and are now heading in your direction, over.'

'Central 42, to control, description please, over.'

'Central 42, three men, one heavily-built wearing a checked sports jacket, a baldy geezer and one slim built. They are on the west footway walking north, over.'

'Central 42, received and I've got them in vision now, over.'

With that I took a series of photographs on my Pentax camera using my 200mm Takumar lens. Others were shot on the Nikon kit.

'Central 42, I have completed my part, do you understand, over?'

'Central 42, received and understood pull out now, over.'

'Central 42, received and out.'

I then drove back to New Scotland Yard and went straight to the dark room to process the film. I had gotten six or seven very good shots. One in particular was a close-up where their faces filled the frame. One of the men, in a sports jacket, was seen to be carrying a ring between his thumb and index finger. I then took the photos to the officers involved.

'Excellent photos, Jim,' they said. 'This one is Sewell and this one is Haynes. We are not sure of the third one, but his name may be Smith. Sewell is the man holding the ring.'

A few days later the same officers informed me that the Hatton Garden team was going to do a job 'up country'. I sat in the canteen with them, and one of the officers was disgusted that they were not being allowed to follow them.

'Jim, we wanted to follow them up north and then hit them on the job, but the Guv'nor has said to let them go, allow them to do the job and then hit them when they come back with the gear.'

'That's exactly what they did on the BSA factory job.' I said. 'There is one thing for sure, C11 knew what was going to happen and they let it go ahead, and we all know why. Someone, someday, is going to get badly hurt. They were lucky nobody was killed on that job.'

The officers finished their tea and left the table. Nobody picked up on my comments, and I had the impression there were certain incidents that were not talked about.

SIXTEEN

WHO DID KILL SUPERINTENDENT RICHARDSON?

What though on hamely fare we dine
Wear hoddin grey, an' a' that
Gie fools their silks and knaves their wine
A man's a man, for a' that
For a' that an' a' that
Their tinsel show an' a' that The honest man,
though e'er sae poor Is king of men for a' that.

Robert Burns

Monday, 23rd August, 1971, was the day that was to change the life of some people forever, including my own. One would be killed, others would be shot, others injured and certain Commanders at Scotland Yard would not get the 'drink' they were expecting.

At about 8.30am, Commander David Clarence Dilley's driver arrived in the C11 car to collect him from his home address in South London and take him to New Scotland Yard. The Commander walked up the driveway and was met by his driver, who loaded his briefcase into the rear of the car. There was little conversation as both men listened to channel six on the Metropolitan Police radio. This channel was reserved for Flying Squad and C11 officers. They arrived at New Scotland Yard about

9.30am.

I was at home loading films into my cameras, preparing for the next observation. I drove my C11 observation van to New Scotland Yard, parked it in the basement and took the lift to the fourth floor office. After signing the office book, I went to the canteen for a cup of coffee with some other officers. It was just another Monday morning. We discussed the events of the weekend. I had spent most of Sunday afternoon at Heathrow airport, awaiting the arrival of two Mafioso who were due in from Holland for a meeting with some London 'business associates'. My task was to obtain covert pictures of their arrival and then join the tail as we followed them to the Dorchester Hotel in Central London and photograph them at the meet.

On the outskirts of Blackpool, Supt. Gerald Richardson was loading his car, preparing to spend his day at the police headquarters. He walked down the driveway, waved goodbye to his wife Maureen, took off his uniform cap and threw it onto the back seat of the car. He got into the driver's seat, blew a kiss to Maureen and drove off.

She would never see him alive again.

He was well thought of in the area and known to most of the business community, not only as an excellent and honest CID officer, but also as a charity worker striving to help the local people through his membership of the local Rotary Club.

In a small flat in the centre of Blackpool, a group of five men were loading firearms in preparation to carry out a well-planned robbery on a nearby jeweller's shop.

The men, all Londoners, were:

Frederick Joseph Sewell, aged 38.

Charles Henry Haynes, 43.

Dennis George Bond, 43.

John Patrick Spry, 37.

Thomas Farrell Flannigan, 43.

They had one thing in common. They were self-confessed villains.

They had kept the jeweller's shop under observation for approximately a week, watching the movements of the four staff. The tools of their trade - bags containing weapons, automatic pistols and sawn-off shotguns - were loaded into a stolen Triumph 2000 car. A bronze Ford Capri, which they had stolen a few days earlier in London, had been driven north and was now parked in a nearby side street. A loaded automatic pistol had been left in the boot. This was to be their insurance if they had any problems.

Some robbery teams at that time would carry firearms as frighteners. Sometimes the pistols would be loaded with blanks and the shot from the shotgun cartridges would be substituted with rice, but not so with this team. They carried fully-loaded weapons. A few years earlier, teams like this would never have considered carrying guns, as they knew that if anyone was killed they would have swung for it. However, our politicians knew better than the public, and voted to do away with the rope. Violent crime with the use firearms increased.

The weather on that 1971 August morning in Blackpool was sunny, with a temperature of 17°C. The town was waking up and recovering from a weekend of visitors to the holiday resort. At the Queen's Theatre, Les Dawson was starring for the season with Dora Bryan. In the Opera House, Ken Dodd was packing them in every night. The Ship and Royal public house at Lytham St Anne's was offering a steak meal for under a pound.

Back in London, Commander Dilley, the officer in charge of C11, had been dropped off on the 'Flight Deck', the area outside the front doors of the Yard. As usual, he took a lift to the fourth floor, walked along the corridor and entered his office. He settled into his swivel director's chair, picked up the phone and dialled four digits.

'Here, Ken, can you pop down and see me?'

He was shortly joined by his old mate, Commander Ken Drury, who was in charge of the Flying Squad. Another senior officer, Commander Wallace 'Wally' Harold Virgo, soon joined them. The office door was closed. After about five minutes, Dilley came out of his office and crossed the corridor to the main C11 office. He put his head round the door, smiled and raised three fingers to his driver, no words were spoken. Mr Dilley wanted three coffees delivered to his office for the meeting.

After a few minutes his driver returned, tray in hand, and knocked on the door. A pair of hands reached out and took the tray into the room filled with smoke and laughter. Once again the door was closed. This meeting was for the 'trusted'.

In Blackpool, on this sleepy Monday morning, the men sat in the stolen Triumph 2000, which they had parked in Queen's Square, close to the junction with the Strand. It was time to do the job.

'OK, got the tools?'

'Yes.'

'Masks?'

All nodded.

'All gloved up?'

'Yes, yup, OK.'

'Let's fucking do it.'

Halfway down the narrow street was Preston's the jewellers, manned by its four staff. The four men walked slowly towards the shop. Two were carrying concealed weapons; at least one pistol and a sawn-off shotgun. The other two were carrying holdalls. As they reached the door they pulled on their stocking masks and crashed in, screaming at the top of their voices.

'Fucking get down you bastards, get fucking down.'

'What? What?' the staff asked in their confusion.

'Fuck you, get on the fucking floor now, you bastards.'

'What?'

'Get on the fucking floor now, or I'll blow your fucking heads off!'

'OK, OK, please don't shoot!'

They've got guns. I've never seen a gun. We're on the floor, how did we get here? These thoughts spun round in the heads of the staff. They were not all on the floor. Unbeknownst to the robbers, the sales manager had moved quietly into a rear office and pressed a silent alarm.

'Here, you two, get up and fill these bags with the Tom,' a robber demanded.

'What's Tom? I've never heard of anything called Tom?' was the reply.

'The fucking jewellery, fill the fucking bags.'

With guns pressed to their heads, the terrified staff filled the holdalls.

The coffee cups were being refilled in the Commander's office. Mr Dilley leaned forward and gently rolled the ash off the end of his large cigar into the crystal ashtray in the centre of his desk. Ken Drury looked over. 'How's the gout Dave?' 'Fucking playing me up,' replied Dilley.

The screaming continued in Preston's the jewellers.

'Fucking move it, never mind the poxy watches, put the fucking diamonds in the bag.'

The silent alarm was sounding at the police station. A radio message had been sent to all cars. Unarmed officers were on their way to Preston's. Was it a false alarm, accidentally triggered by the staff as they opened for business?

In the Commander's office, the coffees and cigars were going down well. These officers were the cream of the CID, and with that they had control of everything, including junior officers' promotions or otherwise. They also had the power to break any officer. They were truly untouchable, particularly Dave Dilley as Commander of the Criminal Intelligence Department. He even had overall control of the telephone intercept department. He knew what was going on in the country.

Walking down the Strand in Blackpool and enjoying the morning sunshine was Mr Ronald Gale, a fire officer. As he strolled towards the jewellers, a woman from a nearby shop ran towards him, yelling, 'Preston's is being robbed. Help, get the Police.'

Gale ran to the jeweller's shop, only to be stopped by a shotgun pointed at his stomach, 'Fucking back off, you bastard, or you will get it.' His automatic reaction was to move his arms slowly out to his sides and up to shoulder level. 'Whoa, whoa, take it easy, OK.'

Before Mr Gale could do or say anything further, a gang member came from behind and hit him over the head with an iron bar. 'Keep your fucking nose out of things... bastard!' Mr Gale didn't hear these words. He dropped to his knees onto the floor, blood running from the head wound, and passed out.

'It's bloody cold in this office Dave; you really ought to get something done with this air-conditioning. My coffee's bloody freezing, I think it's time that cabinet was opened for a livener,'

Drury said.

DD got up and walked over to a metal cabinet, taking the key from his trouser pocket. He unlocked and opened the doors to display his large display of booze and cigars.

'Now you're talking. Have you had it off?' Drury asked.

'Not me, Alex Eist's snout 'stuck up' a lorry-load of mixed booze and his team had them off, couldn't have been better, got them at the slaughter and a little bit of weeding had to be done.'

DD wagged his index finger and gave a wry smile as he poured out the Scotch.

Mr Gale lay still on the pavement. The woman who raised the alarm was screaming and sobbing. This was Blackpool, people don't do armed robberies here.

'Right let's fucking go.'

A gunman bent down and put his masked face near to the staff. They could smell his vile breath and perspiration. In a whisper, he calmly spoke to them: 'Now you lot, no fucking heroics.'

The villains raced out of the shop with the holdalls, jumping over Mr Gale's motionless body.

The shop was suddenly silent, except for the occasional muffled sob.

The staff slowly got up from the floor.

Charles Henry Haynes was waiting with the engine revving in the Triumph getaway car. The four men ran towards him. They were still masked-up. At least one of them was still openly carrying a pistol. A local window cleaner tried to block their escape route. He was knocked to the ground, 'Fuck off, bastard or you're dead.' He looked up from the ground into the working end of a pistol. He froze.

Driving a Panda car in the area was PC Walker, who had just received a radio message alerting him to the robbery. He drove to the Strand just in time to see the four men running from the jewellers and getting into the Triumph. PC Walker drove his Panda car at them and managed to pin one of the robbers against the getaway car. The others started dragging their accomplice into the car.

'It's the Old Bill, go, go!'

'Stop, stop, he's still hanging out of the car.'

'Chas, stop for fuck's sake, stop!'

'Here, take my hand, get in.'

They pulled him into the car as it screeched off.

The Panda car accelerated after it.

'Put the fucking window down.'

One of the robbers stuck a sawn-off shotgun out of the window.

'This'll slow the fucker down.'

It didn't. PC Walker continued to chase the car through the streets of Blackpool for a mile while radioing a commentary back to headquarters. After another few hundred yards he lost sight of the car.

'Bastard, we've lost the bastard, out, get out now!'

They scrambled out carrying the bags of jewellery and ran towards a stolen Ford Capri they had left nearby.

But, as they were about to get into the car Sergeant Walker, now on foot, walked towards them.

'Fuck it, it's that Old Bill, get back into the car.'

Walker continued towards them, his heart beating a tattoo.

The five ran back to the Triumph, its doors were still lying open and the engine still running.

Sewell jumped in behind the wheel. Spry fell into the passenger's seat. The others clambered into the back and they drove off wildly, tyres screeching.

'Fuck him, fuck him!'

Walker got back into the Panda and continued the chase. 'They're still in the Green Triumph Estate... Oscar... Hotel... Mike... 674... E... Echo. They're five up... out of Back Welbeck Street... I'm still with the Triumph... they are armed... at least one pistol and a sawn-off shotgun... over.'

The staff at the control room listened in awe.

'Other units are on way. Keep the commentary going, Carl, over'

'Shit, I've just lost them...'

He soon found them again. They had collided into a garage door and were trapped in an alleyway, preparing to escape on foot.

As Walker began to get out of his car, one of the men walked towards him aiming a pistol. Walker stayed in his car. This was early turn in Blackpool, these things don't happen here. I should have been in for breakfast just now. He sat motionless.

The gunman returned to his car then reversed at high speed, hitting the Panda car which shot across the road leaving a corridor clear for their escape.

'Control, I've been rammed. The car's knackered!'

Other police units were now taking up the chase. One was being driven by a PC Ian Hampson. He got behind the getaway car and continued the chase.

'Oh! Shit another Old Bill car…'

'Where?'

'Behind us, right up our arse!'

Spry looked over his shoulder and into the face of the pursuing officer.

'Hold tight,' Sewell said as he slammed on the brakes. The car came to an abrupt halt. The police car crashed into the back of the Triumph. PC Hampson started to open the door of his smashed car. Spry got out of the Triumph, pistol in hand and walked towards him. As he did so, he coolly pulled up the neck of his red polo neck sweater to cover the lower part of his face. Hampson looked in terror down the barrel of the pistol.

'Big Ken' looked down into his empty glass. 'That'll do me, I've got a lunch with a 'cock' up west.'

And with that he left DD's office.

Spry fired through the glass, hitting Hampson in the chest. The bullet lodged next to his heart. The officer fell into the street. Spry walked calmly back to the getaway, smoking gun in hand.

'Let's fucking move it, that fucking hero's not going any place.'

'Is he dead?'

'Bollocks, move it.'

The car was once again driven off at speed as they resumed their escape. The smell of cordite from the smoking gun filled the car.

A half-finished cigar was smouldering in the ashtray in the Commander's officer. Dilley sat reading through some dockets

Sewell went missing for approximately one week. I have been told that certain officers knew he and his associates were in Lancashire during this time. Indeed, there was a lot of hushed activity in the office and from the conversations I overheard, senior offices, both from the Flying Squad and C11, knew who had committed these offences and knew their addresses.

Officers subsequently arrived from Blackpool and came into the C11 office. I was instructed by David Dilley to show them the usual suspects, but to keep the Hatton Garden photos 'out of the way at this time'.

An officer from Blackpool came to my office, and while showing him the usual suspects, he moved a piece of paper to lean against my desk. He also picked up some photographs, turning them over as he did so.

'Shit, that's the bastard we've got. That one there, that, that one. We've got him in custody, his name's Spry, not Smith... the big bastard is wearing the same jacket as he was wearing when he killed the boss.'

The officer was so filled with emotion that he could hardly get the words out. He took the photographs and said, 'Jim, come down with me to the meeting.'

I said, 'Hold on a minute, give them to me.'

Materials from C11 were not allowed to be shared without the permission of the senior officer in charge of an operation.

He handed the photographs to me and together we walked down to a glass room at the end of the office. Inside were various senior officers from the Flying Squad and Blackpool. He called his boss out of the meeting and showed him the pictures. His boss took the photos and immediately returned to the meeting, closed the door behind him and the last words I heard were, 'That's him, that's the bastard that killed our boss.'

If looks could kill I would have been dead at that point, as Dilley stared at me. Standing next to him was Alex Eist, a senior officer whom many other officers would not work with as he was considered 'dodgy'.

I waited in my office, and somewhere around 9.00pm the photographs were returned to me by Dilley. By now, the three other men had also been positively identified. Their home addresses would certainly have been known to Dilley. He threw the photographs onto my desk and told me to put them somewhere 'out of the road' where no one else could see them.

The next few hours were a charade, as Dilley and company had to hide their previous knowledge of the gang's activities from the Blackpool officers. This included withholding information from them of the home addresses of the three men. It could be argued that this was done, in part, to protect the informant on the gang.

However, I believe that this was a 'business as usual' affair for corrupt officers where criminals were allowed to carry out crimes and then a bogus informant was offered up to receive the reward money from insurance companies. This money was handed to the 'informant' by the insurers. The bogus informant received his fee and the rest of the money was split between police officers in on the scam.

Of course, all this money did not just go to these officers. There had to be a 'divvy up'; there were other people at different departments at the Yard had to be 'looked after'. This would include the most senior officer in the department and the person in the Intercept Office, if an intercept was involved.

This entire process was later confirmed to me by a man who had actually been put up as a bogus informant.

During the four hours he was missing, Sewell had collected his clothes from the home of Barbara Palmer, another woman friend. He told her he would have to 'write her off'.

SEVENTEEN

A TOWN MOURNS ITS CHIEF

The flag at Blackpool Tower was flown at half-mast as a mark of respect for the town's 'Chief.' Eight policemen carried Superintendent Richardson's coffin into St John's Parish Church, where they placed it in front of the altar steps. The coffin was left open at the request of Mrs Richardson. Mr Richardson was dressed in uniform. Thousands joined the queue that filled the stairs into the church and passed the coffin to show their respects.

On 26th August, 1971, Mr Richardson was laid to rest. 100,000 people turned out, shops were closed and staff were given time off to attend. Two minutes' silence were observed and all the fruit machines along the Golden Mile were closed down. The cortege was led by eleven mounted police, followed by the police band. 300 police officers of all ranks marched on either side of the hearse.

At St John's, Mrs Richardson knelt and cried at her 'Gerry's' coffin. They had been married in this church fifteen years before.

Her wreath of red roses lay on the coffin with her message 'Ours was a special kind of love… I will fight for you my love'

During the service, the Rt. Rev A.L.E. Hoskyns-Abrahall described Mr Richardson as 'A greatly-respected officer who had been brutally and callously murdered.' He continued: 'His death is a national tragedy, highlighting as it does those deteriorating standards of behaviour in so many fields which people who ought to know better defend in the name of liberty. This is not the place to discuss what society should do with the violent criminal. The great silent majority who are on the side of law and order must stand up and be counted. We must become more and more vocal in defence of those virtues and standards of behaviour which had once made this nation great.'

Thirty-five years on and still the majority of our politicians have not taken to heart the Reverend's words and the public's thoughts. Why?

Whilst the service was in progress in Blackpool, Flying Squad officers from the Met were racing towards Stoneleigh Abbey in Warwickshire. The Abbey, founded in 1154 by Cistercian Monks, was hosting the National Pony Club championships. Amongst the competitors was Denise Haynes, the daughter of Charles Douglas Haynes. The Squad officers took up observation points around the grounds of the estate.

Just after midday, Haynes drove into the grounds and joined the queue of traffic waiting to pay the entrance fee. As he drove up to the cash booth, he wound down his window and held out his hand with the pound entrance fee in it. Instead of receiving his ticket, his outstretched arm was held by a Flying Squad Officer while another stuck a pistol 'up his nose'.

'Police. Move, and the last thing you will hear in this life is a big fucking bang. You're nicked for killing the Guv'nor in Blackpool.'

With that, Haynes was taken from the car, handcuffed and driven to West End Central Police Station in London and then onto Blackpool, where he was charged.

Unknown to police, Sewell went into hiding in a mid-terrace Victorian flat at 46 Birnam Road, Holloway in North London, where he stayed until he received an early morning wake up call six weeks later.

At 6.45am on the seventh of October, whilst Sewell lay in his 'snore box', police were cordoning off the area. Holloway was shrouded in fog, an ideal morning for the raid. Forty officers, many of them armed, crept quietly round the property. Police dog handlers with their dogs moved in. Mr Mounsey from the Blackpool police, with some officers from Blackpool, together with Met officers including Detective Inspectors George Brothers and John Bland, went to the flat.

They kicked the front door in and rushed up a flight of stairs to a rear bedroom door. Their hearts were pounding against their chests as if trying to burst out. DI Bland stood back and nodded. Officers kicked the bedroom door in. This was no ordinary raid - they were after a man who had killed a colleague and had tried to kill others. They knew, given the chance, he would kill them. In one of the rooms they entered DI Brothers saw a man on the bed. It was Sewell, lying there naked.

'He's here!' Brothers called out.

Sewell turned round and tried to reach under the pillow. Brothers, no stranger to dealing with the slag of this world, dived at Sewell and punched him as hard as he could in the face. This bastard was not going to given the chance to kill any more policemen. He tried to hold Sewell down. The fracas continued as Sewell fought to escape.

Mr Mounsey, gun in hand, stood at the bottom of the bed.

'We are police, if you have a gun, don't touch it.'

Sewell continued fighting. Another two officers piled in.

Sewell still continued fighting. He was eventually restrained, handcuffed and held on the floor. A Flying Squad officer, his pistol now in his shoulder holster, bent down next to the killer's ear and cautioned him.

'Move and you're fucking dead, you brave bastard!'

Sewell lay still, blood running from his face, the officer's words ringing in his ears. The very words he had screamed at the police officers on THAT Monday morning.

The room was torn apart as the officers searched for evidence.

Under the bed was a sawn-off shotgun.

Sewell was arrested and taken to Holloway Police Station, where he was held until 1.00pm. He was then driven back to Blackpool at high speed. During the journey back, Sewell repeatedly told the officers in the car that he had shot Mr Richardson.

At the trial Sewell said, 'I shall see him every day. He was too brave. He just kept coming.'

Another man, Panayiotis Nicou Panayiotou, a twenty-five-year-old Greek, was also taken back to Blackpool. He was charged with hiding Sewell at his property.

Sewell was sentenced to life imprisonment, with a

recommendation that he serve at least thirty years. The others were sentenced to twenty-five and ten years.

The following awards were made:

Superintendent Gerald Richardson: The George Cross, posthumously.
PC Carl Walker: The George Cross and promotion to Sergeant.
Inspector Ken MacKay: The George Medal.
PC Ian Hampson: The George Medal and promotion to Sergeant.
PC Pat Jackson: The George Medal.
Detective Sergeant Andrew Hillis: The George Medal.
Detective Constable Edward Hanley: The British Empire Medal.
Superintendent Edward Gray: The British Empire Medal.
Superintendent Stephen Drummond Redpath: Queen's Commendation.

It is the largest number of George Crosses and George Medals ever awarded for one incident.

For years I tried to find out what the background to this very sad event was, and why my career was cut short in the job I lived for. In a chance meeting in a café, a criminal whom I did not know started to talk about his life in Puerto Banus on the Costa del Sol. After a short while, and with some encouragement from me, he volunteered his connections with none other than Frederick Sewell. He then started to brag about how Sewell had made a fortune in property deals whilst serving his time in prison. He had in fact become a millionaire, and had a property built for him awaiting his release from prison, although he did not have to wait that long. When on day release he visited the chalet-style property being built for him. This also gave him the opportunity to visit another similar property also being built for him.

I have wondered for years about the mystery surrounding the 'Blackpool job'. Why Dilley's reluctance to keep secrets from Blackpool police officers? Why did Dilley and Alex Eist look so worried when confronted with my photograph of the robbers taken a few days before the robbery?

During enquires I have made of retired officers, I am in no

doubt that one of the gang was a 'snout' for one of the senior officers, and this officer knew everything about the planning for the robbery. It is no wonder we were not allowed to follow the 'so-called suspects'.

Things were falling into place.

EIGHTEEN
MRS ROBERTS GOES SHOPPING

During November 1972 I was working with one of the 'Four District' team from C11. The team was led by Detective Inspector Bob Watt and his right-hand man, Detective Sergeant Joe Skillin. I was assisting them in keeping observation on a robbery team in South London. As was usual with Bob's team, when they had finished for the day they would have a briefing in the Tank, the bar in the basement of New Scotland Yard.

We were sitting talking with Bob when he was called away to listen to what an informant had to say. On his return, he sat down with a puzzled smile on his face.

Joe smiled. 'What's going on? He's up to something, Jim, I know that look.'

'I've just got a bit of info from the man. "There's a Robin coming out on a foggy night." What the hell is all that about?'

Bob, a canny Scot from Forfar, always played his cards close to his chest.

'I can assure you my man is not into bird watching, and besides, Robins don't fly in the fog. Is it a code for something? Unfortunately, my man can't tell me.'

Joe looked up from his own bird, the Famous Grouse.

'Robin Hood?'

'It's more likely a Robin Bastard,' said Bob as he leant back in his chair.

We talked this over for a few moments and then Bob supplied us with some more information.

'From what I can gather, there's a bird called Dorothy involved.'

Joe looked up.

'That's a pre-war name. This has got to be an old bird. Where do you think she comes from?'

'I'm not sure, but it will be London. My informant is very iffy, but I should get a bit more tomorrow,' and with that Bob stood up.

The following day we all met up in South London to carry-on with the observation. Within minutes of us starting, Bob received a radio message asking him to contact his man again.

On his return he was deep in thought.

'My man tells me Dorothy has only been trying to get hold of bolt cutters. Who the hell is she, and who the hell is she getting them for? If she's an old bird she's not getting them for herself. The whole thing sounds very iffy. It may be she's dead straight, but we have to find out who she is. But I can assure you, if my man's got an interest, she's up to no good. This isn't straight. What does an old bird, once again assuming she is an old bird, want with bolt cutters?'

On my return to Scotland Yard, I mulled the conversation over in my head, and in the office I spoke to Bob and Joe.

'Guv, I've had an interest in the Foxtrot One One case and I've got a feeling Harry Roberts' grandmother called him Robin. I think she even mentioned it on a TV interview when she appealed for Roberts to give himself up. Yes, I'm sure she did.'

Bob was off his chair and down to the Criminal Records Office. After about twenty minutes he returned carrying a bulging file under his arm. He put it down on his desk. The heading was HARRY MAURICE ROBERTS. Bob had a quick look through it and gave a wry smile. He then locked the file in his drawer and pointed to me.

'Right you... book out to South London, you're with me and Joe. Show 'Observations in the Book'. I'm going to buy you a steak!'

We arrived at The Royal Oak public house in Clapham High

Street. Its specialty was a large steak sitting on a bed of crisps with a grilled tomato on top; we got stuck in!

'We'll make a detective of you one day, Smithy. I know who Dorothy is,' said Bob, with a thankful smile on his face.

'Go on, Guv'nor.'

'It's Harry Roberts' mother, and who did you say Robin was?'

'I think it's Roberts… I'm sure Robin was his Gran's pet name for him.'

Bob raised his glass.

'Spot-on, I'll bet the old cow's going to get him out. Drink up, we're going to stop her farting in church!'

Joe sucked air in through his clenched teeth.

'Nice one my son.'

The following day I was hidden in the back of my observation van watching Dorothy, aged seventy-three, the mother of the evil Harry Roberts, at her home address, a flat in Augustus Street, Camden Town, London. At about 11.00am, as she left, I ran off a few pictures using a Nikon with a 400 mm Nova Flex system. She was followed on foot to Camden High Street in North London.

Was this the woman who had appealed on TV for Robin to give himself up after the killings?

She had a headscarf tied under her chin, her red hair sticking out with a 'kiss curl' hanging over her forehead. She walked down the road with not the slightest idea she was being followed, or that I was photographing her every move. She eventually entered an ironmonger and tool supplier. I followed her in, and just behind me came Joe, who like myself, had been a joiner before joining the Met. We could blend into this environment… we could speak the language.

'Can I help you?' an assistant asked.

I walked over as near to Mrs Roberts as I could without her seeing me and spoke to the man behind the counter.

'Do you have any inch number-eight round-head brass screws?'

'Just a minute,' and with that he walked away.

Joe stood behind me looking at some tools. We could both hear the conversation Mrs Roberts was having with the other shop assistant.

'I don't know what all the measurements mean, they're for a friend.'

She looked puzzled. What an actor.

The elderly shop-assistant was holding an order form in his hand, doing all he could to help the poor old soul.

'It's not the size that's the problem. It's the hardened cutting edges. We are having to have them made up specially. What are they for?'

'Your screws, mate, how many?'

My assistant arrived back and interrupted my listening.

'Just twelve.'

What a time to come back with my order.

He put the screws into paper bag, I paid and walked out. Joe was left to listen to the rest of the conversation. Afterwards, we met up in the coffee shop at Euston Station.

'Well?' said Bob.

'She is buying cutters all right. They have to have specially hardened edges. She has placed an order for them, but that's all I could get. I had to leave.'

I looked at Joe.

'Yeah that's right, Guv'nor,' said Joe.

Once again he breathed in through his clenched teeth and let out a loud sigh.

'The shopkeeper talked about the bolt cutters. I picked him up, saying they would cut through reinforcing rods with no problems. Then she comes out with some old bollocks that they are for her nephew who's working in Scotland and is coming back in a few weeks. The geezer said they should be ready by next week.'

The next week we kept her house in Augustus Street, Camden, under observation. She did not leave the house on many occasions, but when she did it was to do the usual type of shopping.

It was confirmed that Harry Roberts was in Parkhurst Prison on the Isle of Wight.

We could not make an approach to the prison just in case he had inside help; highly unlikely, but no chances could be taken.

On Wednesday, 22nd November, 1972, at about 11.00am, Mrs Roberts left her address. She was followed by us and another member of the team, Detective Sergeant Fred Parish. Fred was born in South London, in the Walworth Road. He became a firemen in the area, and then became a police officer working in the area where he had been born. This was most unusual in the Met, as most of the recruits had come from outside the London area.

Fred was a great practical joker. As CID officers we were required to keep a diary of daily events and expenses. Due to the nature of the work carried out, the entries and locations did not always reflect 'the truth, the whole truth and nothing but the truth'. I wanted the name of a pub to refer to with regards to meeting an informant.

'Anyone know a pub near the Elephant and Castle?' I called out.

Fred looked up from his desk.

'The Ring of Feathers.'

'Cheers, Fred,' and with that I neatly printed in my diary THE RING OF FEATHERS and neatly underlined it. The office was silent.

'Fred, where is The Ring of Feathers?'

I waited, pen in hand.

'Round the duck's arse!'

The office exploded in laughter.

I spent the next ten minutes trying to erase my last entry.

Dressed in overalls, Fred followed Mrs Roberts down the road and straight in to the ironmongers.

'Good morning love, oh, yes, I remember you. You've come about the cutters?' the assistant asked.

How could the assistant not remember her, dressed in a waterproof coat and flat shoes, complete with a headscarf? She didn't exactly blend into the shop. She looked at him.

'Are they ready?'

'Came in this morning, love.'

Fred stood as close to her as he could and ordered a broom. Not just any broom. It had to be a special size!

'How long are the shafts, guv?'

The shop assistant looked him up and down.

toilet was a cupboard. When this was searched, the bolt cutters were found in a bucket with a floor mop draped over them.

Roberts' cell, number 218, was searched. His bed was removed, and behind the head of the bed it was noticed that two small holes had been drilled in what appeared to be plaster. These holes were large enough to allow a darning needle to get through. It was soon to be discovered that this 'plasterwork' was in fact plywood fitted into the plaster and painted. It was undetectable apart from the two small holes, which were, in fact, keyholes. A small piece of metal was inserted into these holes and turned. The plywood, measuring approximately 20 inches by 20 inches, could then be removed. This revealed a tunnel, where 20 courses of bricks had been removed, leaving another two inches of brickwork on the outside of the prison.

This could have been pushed out, and would have given access onto a flat roof and freedom for the killer. Inside the tunnel was found a pair of sunglasses, a compass, a pair of wire cutters, a short-bladed dinner knife with a sharpened end, a homemade wooden brace, some drill bits, a gas lighter, newspaper cuttings containing maps of the Isle of Wight, a list of addresses, a business reply card containing details of replica guns, a file, and four five-pound notes. An imitation pistol was also found. This had been made from shoe leather and dyed black. In dimmed lighting there is no doubt this imitation could easily have been mistaken for the real thing. The most sinister thing found was a list of witnesses who had given evidence at his trial. Some of the names had been highlighted.

In the tunnel between the brickwork were found steel re-enforcing rods, which had been inserted during construction and were waiting to be cut. We had no doubt that these were what the cutters was for.

Mrs Roberts appeared at Winchester Crown Court on 21st March 1973, where she pleaded Not Guilty to helping her son in a plot to escape from Parkhurst Prison. She pleaded Not Guilty to taking a pair of cutters into the prison on 30th November the previous year with intent to facilitate the escape of Harry Roberts.

It was disclosed at the trial that it would have taken Roberts two to three months to construct the tunnel, which had been his second attempt to escape by the same means.

Mrs Roberts was represented by John Mortimer QC. When giving evidence, she wept as she told of her fortnightly visits to the Isle of Wight to take her son a little food and cigarettes. She said, 'I visited him because he is my son, but he did not confide in me. He used to say I was too old.'

In his closing speech for the defence, Mr Mortimer said: 'He had collected a veritable armoury of escape equipment without her help. Are we to believe he needed the help of a septuagenarian, arthritic cook to come hobbling in with one of the implements?'

Despite the wealth of evidence that Bob Watt's team had collected, the Hampshire Police, for reasons best known to them, never called any Met Officer to give evidence in this case. The jury found Mrs Roberts Not Guilty.

After serving 48 years in prison, Roberts was released in November 2014.

His fellow robber, Duddy, died in prison in 1981.

Witney was released from prison on licence in 1991. He went to live in Bristol, where, in 1999, he was found dead in his home. He had been bludgeoned to death with a hammer by his flatmate, a heroin addict.

NINETEEN

ANOTHER GUN

Shortly after Mrs Roberts' trial Eric Turner, a Detective Constable at C11, and I had been out on an early morning observation at a property in North London.

As usual after an 'early one' we went to a greasy-spoon café at the rear of Oxford Street. After breakfast we returned to the observation van. We drove down Park Lane towards Hyde Park Corner. It was a bright summer morning. We were chatting and making comments on events which were coming over on the Police radio. Traffic was comparatively quiet. I had the driver's window down.

As we stopped at the traffic lights a small van pulled up alongside us on Eric's side. I glanced to my left and saw the van driver, a man of about twenty-five years of age, indicating that he wanted to speak to us. He did not know we were police officers, as we were in an unmarked van and were wearing builders' overalls.

'Eric, the guy on your left wants to talk to you. Do you know him?'

'I've never seen him in my life.'

And with that Eric wound down the window.

'Yes, mate?'

'Where's Buckingham Palace, mate?'

'Straight over the roundabout, you can't miss it.'

The traffic lights changed to green and I was about to drive off.

'Hoy!'

It was the driver of the van. We both looked to our left. The driver had a pistol sticking out of the window.

We ducked down.

'What the?!' Eric shouted.

Bang, bang!

'Shit!'

'You okay?' we spoke in unison.

'Yes, okay. What was that all about?' I asked.

The van driver took off, his tyres screeching. I accelerated after him. Eric grabbed the radio microphone.

'MP, urgent message from Central 42.'

'All units stand by. Go ahead, Central 42'

'MP from Central 42, we have just been shot at by the driver of a Ford Escort van. We have no injuries.'

There was no panic in Eric's voice as he calmly read out the registration number of the van.

'Central 42, keep up the commentary.'

'We are now in Constitution Hill, 60 miles per hour, travelling south, now past the front of 'Buck House'.'

'Central 42, other units are on their way. There is nothing known on the vehicle, over.'

'MP from Central 42. Past the Royal Mews, Straight on over red ATS. He's turning right, travelling north towards Knightsbridge.'

'All received, Central 42.'

'MP He's stopped in traffic outside the Westminster Bank'

Eric was out of our vehicle, followed by myself. We were on automatic pilot. Eric pulled the driver's door open and punched the driver full on the face. I had come in the passenger's door and had him in a neck lock. We were both shouting 'Police' as Eric pulled him out by the wrists with me following. I had my hands over his eyes as I 'assisted' him out of the van. We spread-eagled him on the pavement. Our main aim was to keep his hands away from the gun sticking out of the waist band of his trousers.

The welcoming sound of the familiar two-tone sirens of the approaching police grew louder as our colleagues approached. Police cars seemed to be all around us, their crews running towards us, truncheons in hand.

Eric had pulled the gun out of the driver's trousers and put it on the footway, out of reach. Pedestrians were cowering in doorways. A bank had slammed its doors shut.

In an incident like this the approaching Police are just as likely to hit first and ask questions later. Our prisoner was now face down on the pavement, Eric's foot on the back of his neck and mine on his outstretched right arm. We both managed to get our warrant cards out in time to save our skins from approaching colleagues.

Blood was on the footway from the prisoner's nose. He was pulled to his feet and held against his van.

The familiar sound of the police officer's voices could be heard above the traffic.

'Right folks, move along, the show's over!'

Show? It turned out to be more of a farce.

'Right the van's here, let's get him in it and see what we've got,' Eric said.

The prisoner was 'walked off' to the police van. An inspector walked over and picked up the gun from the footway. We stood with our hands on our knees, our backs against the prisoner's van. We were struggling to get our breath back. The inspector walked over to us.

'Can I have word, gents?'

'Yeah, sure, Guv.'

'This pistol's a replica, it's been made to fire blanks.'

We both looked at each other in disbelief. Two minutes earlier we both thought that someone was going to kill us.

We both walked over to the police van and opened the door.

'What's your game, arsehole?'

The prisoner looked at us, dried blood on his face.

'I'm sorry, it was only a joke. I didn't know you were police. Sorry.'

'Driver, take him to the nick.'

We slammed the van door shut and the van drove off. The inspector looked at the gun.

'Somebody is going to get killed one of these days, with prats pissing about with these things, and then Old Bill will be left to pick up the pieces. See you at the nick, gents.'

The van driver, aged about twenty-five, to this day will probably never realize how lucky he is to be alive.

Eric, a trained 'shot', frequently carried a firearm when we went out together on jobs. The particular job we had just finished did not justify him carrying that particular morning.

A few months later Eric and I were in Bournemouth looking for suspects involved in the shooting of a Police officer. We were driving in the town centre when we came across a police officer being attacked by a group of men. We ran over to assist the officer, who was struggling with a prisoner. As we were putting the prisoner on the ground, another man ran over and scissor-kicked Eric in the face. In my statement I described how his face 'exploded in a mass of blood'. He was rushed to hospital and was admitted to intensive care, where he remained for three weeks.

Fortunately he survived, but it was over a year before he was able to return to work. The men responsible were arrested and served long prison sentences.

TWENTY

EVERY BREATH YOU TAKE
I'LL BE WATCHING YOU

It started out as a normal day in my office, situated on the fourth floor in New Scotland Yard, Diaries to be written, photographs to be indexed and stored for future use. The time was fast approaching to walk round the corner to the canteen with a couple of colleagues and discuss events of the previous day. It was at this point my telephone rang.

The call was from a divisional officer, who relayed the following story to me.

Two nights earlier he had been drinking in a local pub in the Bayswater area of London. At the bar were a number of Australian males, in company with two 'stunning females'. He was aware that a gang of Australian shoplifters were operating in England, and these people seemed to fit the bill. Standing next to them was a tall, well-dressed man in his thirties. After some time they all left together.

The officer decided to follow the well-dressed man, as he had split from the others outside the pub. Was this just a 'hunch'? - a feeling police officers are not allowed to act on these days without filling in report after report, asking permission to act, and if this was outside health and safety regulation the action would not be approved.

The officer had followed the man to a house in nearby Moscow Road.

A few days later I was in Moscow Road, hidden in the rear of my observation van. The time was approximately six o'clock; dawn had just broken when I had left home. It was a beautiful summer's morning, with the usual keep fit fanatics jogging towards Hyde Park on the opposite side of Bayswater Road. The temperature in the back of the observation van was rising as the sun got up.

At about eight o'clock, a male aged about thirty to thirty-five years old, six feet tall, left the terraced house. He was smartly-dressed in a suit and carrying a brown A4-sized envelope in his hand. I took a series of photographs as he left and walked away from me. On reaching a Porsche sports car parked at the edge of the pavement he stopped and looked about, as he unlocked the passenger door and dropped the envelope into the car. After closing and locking the door he walked back towards me. This gave me the opportunity to get full frontal images. My driver and I decided to follow him as he boarded a London bus heading towards Oxford Street.

At the famous Selfridges store he got off the bus and crossed to the south side of the street. I jumped out of the van and followed him into Balderton Street. After a short walk he entered an office block on the left hand side of the street. He spoke to what appeared to be a security officer, showed some form of ID and made his way past the security barrier and into the main building.

It was obvious, or so I thought, that we had picked the wrong guy.

It was time for a bit of breakfast in a local café and then back to New Scotland Yard.

I had only been at my desk for a short while when I received a telephone from a senior officer in Special Branch upstairs in the Yard. I had known this officer for some time.

'Jock, fancy a coffee in the canteen?'

I knew for him to invite me for coffee there was something afoot.

'Yes, okay when?'

'Ten minutes. See you then.'

I walked round the corner, through the swing doors to the restaurant and sat down with my coffee. After a few minutes the Special Branch man arrived. I will call him 'George'.

'I suppose you are wondering what this is all about Jock?'

'Yes, well, and I don't suppose you will tell me the full story, best I don't know?'

'Well it is a little bit like that. You were in Moscow Road this morning and followed a guy off. What exactly were you doing there?'

'Just a little bit of an observation on what I thought was one of the Aussie gang. It turned out our information was duff. I followed him off to an office block in Balderton Street where he walked in and passed security, and at that point I left. I don't know what the company is, I can always go back and find out if you want?'

'No that's okay, I know the company. Did you do any pictures of him?'

'Yes, I have a few but I haven't processed them yet.'

'When can you do them?'

'I can have them in the next couple of hours, is it that urgent?'

'That would be brilliant if you can. Who were you working for?'

'No one really, I am trying to build up an album of an Aussie team who are tearing quality outlets apart.'

George thought for a short time and took out his pen and wrote down his extension number on a note pad removed a page and handed it to me.

'Have you made any entries in any books or your diary saying where you were?'

'No, not yet.'

'Don't put anything on paper. Do not worry, I will cover you. I will explain later. When you have the pictures don't show them to anyone and keep the negatives safe. Then give me a call on this number and we can meet up.'

I processed the pictures they; were as described. They showed the guy coming out of the house and then dropping off the envelope into the car. They were all sharp and he could be easily identified, likewise the envelope.

I telephoned George.

'I've got your pictures. They are all okay, about twenty in all.'

'Excellent, I will make a call and I'll get back to you in a couple of minutes.'

After a few minutes my phone rang.

'Jock, I'll see you in the canteen in about five minutes. Don't bring the pictures or the negatives, put them safe and out of sight.'

I arrived in the canteen. George was sitting on his own next to the window. On the table in front of him was a brown large envelope.

'I didn't order you anything to eat, you had a big enough breakfast to last you all day. Jock, you get yourself into some funny things. You are not in any trouble. What I am going to tell you can't go any further. The truth is the people from "box" (MI5/6) were carrying out some work in the area where you were. They were surprised, to say the least, when you turned up. The building you followed the guy to is the American Intelligence building. I can't go into it any further. What I want you to do is go to Trafalgar Square at one o'clock and stand next to the Police Post on the south east corner of the square. Take the pictures and negatives with you in this envelope. A woman will approach you; she will say something like 'Hello Jim, let's have a walk'. Give her the envelope and that's it, your job is done, that's all.'

'That's all, how will she know me?'

'Don't worry, she will know you - she had breakfast with you this morning.'

With that he handed me the envelope, smiled and walked off.

'I'll be in touch when you get back.'

I went back to my office, removed the pictures and negatives from a drawer and put them in the envelope. I then made my way to Trafalgar Square, where I stood next to the Police Post, a circular granite building built at the time the Square was constructed. I had been standing there for a couple of minutes when a woman who could have been my elderly aunt came from behind me.

'Hello Jim, you okay?'

'Yes fine, suppose we should go for a walk, or is that your line?'

'Okay, let's go.'

We walked round the Square, just talking about everything and anything, just passing the time of day.

'Is that my envelope?'

I handed her the envelope. I remember saying to her, 'Been doing this long?' She never looked at me but replied, 'Hundreds of years,' and with that she turned and walked off. I never saw her again.

On my return to the office George phoned and thanked me, and that was the end of that.

Or so I thought.

Some three months later I received a phone call from George asking me to meet him for lunch at the US Embassy in Grosvenor Square in central London at twelve noon. "What now?" I thought to myself, as I walked to the Embassy through St James's Park.

On my arrival I stood on the front staircase - not a thing you can do these days! After a few minutes George appeared from inside the building, in company with another man. Both were wearing identity tags. George introduced him to me as an FBI agent.

We walked into the entrance area, where I signed in and was issued with a visitor's identity tag. Another man was waiting next to the reception desk.

'Hi, Jim I'm Rod. George has told me all about you. My great grandfather came from Scotland, I'm from the Macintosh Clan. Let's go to the restaurant, two of my colleagues have booked a table. They're waiting for us.'

We walked to the restaurant and made our way over to the reserved table, where the other two Americans introduced themselves to me.

'Here Jim, you sit here, we have kept this chair for you.'

I sat down. Rod handed me a menu.

He spoke in a very soft voice.

'Jim, my colleagues are involved in a very active investigation. They have chosen this table as they would like you to watch people coming into the restaurant. If you should recognise anyone just tip me the wink, okay?'

After a few minutes a group of US Naval officers arrived, all wearing uniforms, some with more 'scrambled egg' on their sleeves than others. They were laughing amongst themselves.

I immediately recognised one of them. He was the man from Moscow Road in my photographs.

'The guy sitting down now, he is the man.'

Rod wiped his mouth with his napkin and whispered.

'The guy sitting on the right with his back to us, correct?'

'Yes, that's your man.'

Rod placed his napkin on the table and looked at me.

'Yes that's him, without a doubt.'

'Thanks Jim, enjoy your meal.'

After the meal I was taken to the front door. Rod took my ID card, we shook hands and I left the building. The two FBI men, or whatever they were, remained at the table as I had left.

I walked back to the Yard, tossing all the past events over in my head.

What was it all about? It would be another year before I got some of the answer.

I was in the Tank, the bar on the ground floor in Scotland Yard, sitting on my own when I saw George coming towards me.

'What would you like to drink?'

'Nothing thanks, I'm waiting for some of the team. We're going out on a job. By the way, can you say anything about that American job?'

'Well, yes, but it's secret. Got yourself in the middle of it without realising. The envelope you saw getting dropped off contained secrets of some sort. The car, I think it was a Porsche, was a dead letter box belonging to who knows who. I guess the Yanks know.'

Did George not know who the owners of the dead box were? I don't think so.

'So what happened to the Yank? I suppose I'll be getting called to court some day?'

George looked and smiled.

'No, you will never be required in court. The Yank got posted to Vietnam, where he died in action.'

With that my colleagues arrived and we went out on another mundane job - or so I hoped!

TWENTY-ONE

MUNICH FUN AND GAMES

Robbery and blackmail were keeping us busy at C11. Some of the blackmailers were very ingenious, however one job that did stand out for the sheer speed and audacity of planning by the organizer was during the time of the Munich Olympic Games.

I was called to a briefing at West End Central Police Station on 30th August 1972. The wife of a solicitor, whose husband and son were visiting the Munich Olympic Games, returned home from work to find an envelope containing a typewritten note, which read:

'WE HAVE YOUR HUSBAND AND SON IN MUNICH. UNLESS YOU PUT £10,000 IN A CASE WHICH YOU WILL BUY FROM THE SHOP AT THE CORNER OF HAMPSTEAD ROAD AND DRUMMOND STREET. IT IS IN THE CORNER WINDOW THE CASE HAS A WHITE STRIPE ON IT. PUT THE MONEY IN THE CASE AND HAVE A BOY UNDER 16 YEARS OF AGE HOLDING IT OUTSIDE THAMES TELEVISION ON THE EUSTON ROAD AT EXACTLY 2PM THIS AFTERNOON. WE WILL HAVE A YOUNG MESSENGER COLLECT IT. IF ANY- ONE TRIES TO STOP HIM THEY WILL BE SHOT DEAD.'

She had no way of contacting her husband or son, and there were only four hours before the handover was due to take place. Our impression was that this was a well-organized kidnapping.

However, it was unusual that such a small amount of ransom money was being demanded. The handover point and the shop selling the case were 300 yards apart, suggesting that the kidnappers had local connections.

We chose the youngest-looking trainee at the Police College to be the handover boy. At the briefing he was totally bewildered, as just a week before he had been a shoe salesman and had not even had his 'Hendon haircut'.

An officer went to the shop at Hampstead Road and purchased the case. It was brought back to the briefing, filled with telephone directories and locked.

At 1.55pm, the boyish-looking recruit stood in position with the case between his legs. I was inside a television company's reception area, looking out through the smoked-glass window with a Nikon camera hung round my neck.

At exactly 2.00pm, a spotty-faced boy of about sixteen walked past 'our man'. He casually took the case without breaking his stride and continued along the road.

Along with other officers, I followed him as he headed towards Regent's Park Underground Station. At the station we were down to three officers following him, the other five having lost sight of him because of the traffic. He got into the lift to go down to the trains. I ran down the spiral staircase and stood on the platform. Our target got out of the lift and boarded a train going south. One officer got into the same carriage as him, while Detective Sergeant 'Dougie' Bowles, one of C11's best surveillance officers, and I got into carriages either side. As the train pulled into Elephant and Castle station, the youth attempted to open the locked case, without success. This was our first indication that he might be a 'loner'.

On reaching Tooting Bec Station he got off and started to run up the staircase. I handed my camera to Dougie and ran up the stairs behind him. He ran out of the station into Upper Tooting Road and turned left into Daffrone Road. I ran round the corner after him. When he stopped and looked over his shoulder, I hit him with the full force of my feet in the small of his back. He fell to the ground still clutching the case. I managed, more by luck than good guidance, to land on top of him and pull his arms up his back. There was a crack as I wrenched his arms even further up. I was sweating, the saliva was foaming at my mouth.

'Go for your gun and I'll break your bloody arms, you're nicked!'

'I don't have a gun,' he said.

I lay on top of him as passersby gathered round watching. Within seconds, Dougie arrived and helped me to search him. He didn't have a gun. However, unbeknownst to us, he had broken his collarbone as he fell. A Panda car arrived and we bundled him into the car.

Back at the Police Station he admitted everything, telling us the most amazing story. The previous afternoon, while watching television, his mother had returned from her cleaning job. The Olympics were on the television and his mother casually mentioned that the woman whose house she had been cleaning had seen a close-up of her son and husband 'on the box' in the Olympic Stadium the day before. The woman then went on to say they would be in Germany for the next few days.

From these remarks, her son, a sixteen-year-old schoolboy, had put together his plot to get £10,000 - all within the space of about eight hours. We recovered from a cupboard in his house the typewriter and paper that the ransom note had been typed on.

He was charged, appeared in court, and was given a custodial sentence.

I was investigated after the supposed-kidnapper's solicitor alleged that I had used too much force while arresting his client.

You couldn't make it up!

TWENTY-TWO

TERRORIST RAID ON THE INDIAN HIGH COMMISSION

The traffic in the City of London was at a crawl as I made my way to Scotland Yard in my observation van.

It was 27th February, 1973. The Thames Flood Barrier scheme was under construction, and the walls along the Embankment were being made higher. It had been like this every morning for weeks.

I turned off the Embankment and made my way towards the Savoy Hotel. Over the radio came the call, 'All Central units go to Channel one. India House, the Aldwych, armed robbery taking place now.'

Within a minute I was outside the front door of the Indian High Commission. I stopped my vehicle and got out. Huddled in a doorway outside the Commission were a group of people, one of whom had a gash to the side of her head next to her ear; blood was everywhere. The group were screaming and shouting in their native tongues.

'I'm a Police officer, what has happened?' I asked.

'Men with guns, knives and big swords Sir, they have our friends inside.'

'How many?' I asked.

'Four, five, they are all wearing masks, they have tied people to chairs they are going to kill them.'

I ran back to my van and knelt down at the open passenger's

door, and sent a message to the Information room at the Yard.

I could see through a window into a front room where the hostages were. A masked man was posted at the window. He struck the window with a large sword, and there was a terrific crash as the plate glass came out and smashed onto the ground about ten feet from me, together with a broken piece of the sword. He stood at the hole where the window had been, and behind him I could see a group of hostages.

With a stocking pulled over his face, he was shouting and screaming in some foreign language while holding the broken sword in one hand and a pistol in the other. He pointed the gun straight at me and then started shouting in English that we were going to die for the cause. What cause, I thought?

'I'm a Police officer. Drop your weapons!' I said.

My statement had no effect whatsoever, and he continued screaming that we would all die.

I remembered Fred Gamester, a PC at Poplar, telling me that when he was in the Commandos during the war a 'Jock' from Glasgow used to shout 'Bastard' when they were in battle. Fred reckoned that there was no other accent that could say it in such a way as to instil fear into people. It was worth a try.

I went into Rab C. Nesbitt mode, using some choice language, none of which seemed to assist in the discussions and certainly would not have impressed Wee Francis, my Sunday School teacher from years before.

He kept shouting that I was going to die, and I kept shouting back at him, 'Baastaard, you fucking wee shite!'

We made a fine pair. This was not exactly the kind of negotiating skill one would use today.

As he ranted and raved, he was running back and forth to the hostages and holding the gun to their heads. Hearing gunshots from somewhere inside the building, I grabbed a small CID truncheon and a pair of handcuffs from the van. Going into the street with arms outstretched, I managed to stop the oncoming cars.

As I ran back towards the smashed window, a Traffic Patrol Land Rover arrived. I shouted to the driver and his female passenger, a traffic warden, that the people inside the building had guns. They both bundled out of the passenger's side of the vehicle and lay on the ground. The warden's skirt was round her waist and she appeared to pass out for a short time, then coming to and frantically pulling down her skirt and shouting, 'Help, they can see my knickers!' I guess she was in shock.

More shots were fired from inside the building. I could now see a row of people inside, some with blood on them, tied to chairs. This was a nightmare. It might be trite to say, but everything seemed to be happening at once. And five minutes before, I had been fed up with the traffic.

A man jumped out through the broken window. I noticed he was holding something in his clenched fists. He ran towards me and I punched him as hard as I could in the side of his head. He spun round and fell to the ground. I held my truncheon across his throat, pressing down with both hands. I looked at his hands, they were tied together. He was one of the hostages.

What do you say to a man who has been held hostage, threatened with death, has escaped through an open window, only to be punched in the side of the head and then nearly throttled?

'I am a Police officer, who are you?' I asked.

He mumbled something about 'Secretary to the Commission'.

'I'm sorry about that, I didn't know who you were, how's your head?' I asked.

He answered with a very distinct Indian accent words which I will never forget: 'Oh dear, Sir, okay, okay. Today it is a pleasure to be hit by a British Policeman.'

While I was thus engaged at the front of the building, two of my former colleagues from the Group, PCs George Burrows and Stanley Conley, were entering the building from the rear. Both were armed, as they were on special duties in central London.

The two men ran up a rear staircase, revolvers drawn. As they reached a set of double doors they could hear shouting and screaming coming from the other side. They gently pushed open the door to see a masked man pointing a pistol at them and threatening to kill them. Another masked man, pistol in hand, was threatening to kill the hostages. The officers continually shouted that they were armed and told the men to drop their weapons. The warnings went unheeded, and both officers opened fire. One of the gunmen fell to the floor, fatally wounded.

Conley then crawled along the floor, using the furniture as cover. The other gunman, using a pillar as cover, threatened to kill Burrows. Undeterred, both officers carried on with Burrows giving covering fire from the doorway. Conley was now in a position where he could see the gunman clearly and shouted 'Drop that gun.' The gunman turned and pointed his weapon at Conley. In fear of his life, Conley fired one shot and the gunman fell to the ground. He too was dead.

While this was going on I climbed in through the glassless front window, where I could hear shots and screams coming from inside. My original masked man, now armed with a commando-type knife, was struggling with members of staff. I hit him with my truncheon and down he went. I searched him for weapons in a manner I had never done before. I ripped all of his clothes off down to his underpants. I handcuffed him to myself and jumped out of the window frame, dragging him with me. He was still wearing his mask. I threw him into the rear of the Police Land Rover and we raced off to Bow Street Police Station, where he was detained.

The group carrying out the raid on the India High Commission was comprised of Pakistani teenagers. When the firearms were later examined they were found to be replicas. The boys had not been able to obtain firearms, but had come up with a plan to get possession of them. At college, they made up an acid concoction which was put into a 'Tudor' garden spray. When pressurized by pumping the handle, the sprayer could project the contents up to a distance of twenty feet. They were aware that pointing guns, albeit replicas, at the Police would result in armed officers attending the scene. Their plan was to spray the officers with the acid, blind them and then take their weapons. Had they succeeded with this part of their plan, their intention was then to take the hostages to Heathrow airport and fly them to Pakistan.

I always believed there were more than three people involved in the incident. This was based on those who spoke to me when I arrived at the scene. They stated they saw four or five people inside the building. I heard gunshots before Burrows and Conley arrived, and these could have been blanks as the replicas were suitable for firing caps. The recovered guns had never been fired.

It would seem that there was some high-level diplomatic pressure brought to bear in connection with this incident. A couple of hours after I took my prisoner to Bow Street, two Foreign Office officials made an appearance. When this sixteen-year-old of Pakistan origin appeared in court, he pleaded guilty to various minor offences, and was immediately deported.

Some months later, a senior Special Branch officer met me in Scotland Yard.

'You were correct, Jim, five people did go to India House that day. Two of them came back yesterday, this time with real guns. They were stopped by the officers on the door. The guns were taken and they, with the consent of their families, have been sent back to Pakistan. They admitted to being there the day the other two were killed.'

A few weeks after the incident at India House, George Burrows and Stanley Conley would save the Metropolitan Police from what would have been the biggest loss of life in its history.

They had just arrived in their carrier outside the Yard. There was a rail strike that day, and consequently all car parking was free. They watched as two men parked a car on a meter outside the Yard. One of the men put money into the meter and walked off with his passenger. Both vanished into the crowds in Victoria Street.

Both officers' suspicion was aroused by the man putting money into the meter. The car was examined, and found to contain a large IRA bomb which would have been capable of destroying most of Scotland Yard and the surrounding buildings.

Many were saved from death and serious injury by the diligence of these two men, who had simply seen a man feed a meter on a day when all parking was free.

TWENTY-THREE
AQR

In early 1973 the Metropolitan Police introduced AQRs (Annual Qualification Reports). A new Detective Superintendent had been posted to C11, Detective Superintendent Frank Lovejoy, who was known throughout the CID as 'Little Legs'.

I had seen him around the building and, of course, I had known of him from his involvement in the arrest of the people involved in the BSA (British Small Arms) robbery all those years before, but we had never spoken. I had an appointment to see him in his office to be assessed as to my ability as a police officer.

He handed me the assessment, which he had prepared. When I read it, I could not believe what he had written. Apparently, I was virtually a waste of space in his opinion. I refused to sign the paper.

He pointed out to me that refusal to sign was a disciplinary offence. I agreed to sign it on the basis that I had read the report, not that I agreed with the contents.

I was convinced I had upset him in some way. Throughout my service, no one had ever threatened me with any disciplinary proceeding. Was he annoyed because I had been talking about the BSA job, or the killing of Superintendent Richardson?

The only thing that I had noticed which was amiss was that Keith, my sole colleague in the Photographic Section, had been distancing himself from me, only speaking as and when it necessary. Idle as he was, there was one thing for sure - he was not corrupt.

Despite the setback of my AQR, I carried on as usual. Nothing appeared to substantially change.

TWENTY-FOUR

MARCH 1974.
WHAT'S IT ALL ABOUT?

'Jock, the Guv'nor wants to see you.'

I got up from my desk, put on my jacket and walked down to Dave Dilley's door. It was open. The air conditioning was struggling to cope with the smoke from his cigar.

'Ah, Jock, come in and shut the door.'

I'm thinking to myself, another confidential enquiry?

'Shut the door, Jock, sit down.'

I walked over to the desk. In the large ashtray lay a large Havana cigar, smoke curling up from it.

Dave Dilley's face changed to a serious look.

'I've got good news and bad news for you, my son. The bad news first, is that we are going to lose you.'

'How do you mean?'

I was thinking to myself I must be going to the Bomb Squad. I had been doing a lot of work for them recently.

'Let me tell you the good news, Romford is going to gain from your experience. You're going back to uniform.'

'What?'

'I'm sorry we are losing you, the powers that be think you would be better in uniform at Romford.'

'What powers?'

'It came from above.'

'Who?'

'I can't tell you.'

'Why?'

'They have decided.'

'Who are 'they'?'

He picked up his cigar, drew on it and let the smoke drift out of his mouth. He just stared at me.

'I'll ask you again, who are they?'

'The powers that be.'

'What powers? You're the Guv'nor.'

'You will be leaving us in about a month's time.'

'Romford. Romford, you've just approved the purchase of my new house in South Croydon. I can't work in Romford and live in Croydon. You know that we've got to live within eight miles of the nick.'

'Yes, it's not good news, we'll miss you.'

'Miss me! What have you done to keep me here?'

'It's out of my hands.'

'This is you, isn't it, because I opened my mouth and spoke up about you and Bernie Silver and the Blackpool saga.'

'What?'

'Well, you know, when Bernie Silver was sitting next to you at the top table at the C11 stag do. He was there as your guest. Do you remember it was at the Oval? A villain like that and you let him see all our faces, the photos of Silver and his big mate you took out of the system. What exactly is your game?'

He stared at me, held his cigar up to his mouth, drew on it and rolled his eyes back. He blew the smoke out.

'That's all, you'll be going in a month,' he said.

'No, I'm sorry, I want to know why.'

'That's all.'

And with that he got up, and walked round his desk.

He put his hand in the small of my back and started to usher me out of his office.

'Don't touch me, I don't want your hands touching me. I'll find out why you've done me up like a kipper.'

Any honest officer would have pulled me back into the office and put me up against the door. Not DD. I had hit a very raw nerve.

I walked into the C11 office, my face was white, my legs like jelly. As I did so, Dilley said in a loud voice for all to hear.

'Sorry, Jock, your cover's blown.'

I just looked at him, shook my head, picked up the keys for my van and drove out of Scotland Yard. I drove down to Southwark Police Station where I saw Dave Woodland, a former detective inspector who had been returned to uniform on the instructions of Dilley shortly after the arrests of the Australians. I told him my story.

'Jim, you're a threat to him. Be careful, he'll fit you up. Here, come with me.'

And with that we went down to his office. He took Form 728 from the filing cabinet, and typed the following :

30th March 1973
Detective Chief Superintendent.

In accordance with the above quoted section in General Orders, I request an interview with the Commissioner of Police.

The reasons for this application are confidential but are indirectly related to my previous employment at C11 and my forthcoming transfer from specialist duties.

'Jim, put that in to him and keep a copy. His bottle will go with that, but be very careful, you've discussed DD with one person too many and someone 'bubbled' you up to the man.'

I had no idea who that person could be. Over the years, numerous matters were discussed over a cup of tea in the canteen. Occasionally corruption came up as a topic, but was never named as such. Suspect officers were referred to as 'dodgy'.

I went home feeling that my career was finished.

The next morning I handed the Form 728 to the office clerk. He read it, raised his eyebrows and looked at me.

'Are you sure?'

'Absolutely, give it to him.'

Days passed. I was still doing my job.

After a few days Dave Dilley came into the office, raised his right hand and beckoned me by screwing his index finger up and down. I walked towards him.

In a loud voice he said, 'Yes, Jock, I've got your meeting next Thursday at 2.00pm. That's the one to meet the Commissioner, but you will have to go to see the DAC Jock Wilson first.'

DAC Jock Wilson had been in charge of Special Branch. I had worked closely with him when we were working in Wales during the events leading up to the investiture of Prince Charles. I felt he was a man I could trust.

Thursday arrived and I made my way to DAC's office.

'Come in, sit down Jock. What can I do for you?'

'Well, I've applied to see the Commissioner.'

'Yes, I see that. What's it all about?'

'I prefer to tell the Commissioner, Sir.'

'It's OK, you can tell me and I'll relay any grievances you have to him and we'll get this matter sorted out.'

'No thanks, I want to see the Commissioner personally.'

'Well, that's not the way it works.'

'What?'

'You tell me and I relay it to him. Then if he wants to see you he'll give the OK, and he'll ask to see you.'

'Well, with respect, Sir, that's not how it works. Any officer can have an interview with the Commissioner on a one-to-one basis, as referred to in G.O. Section 6, Para 6 (2).'

This conversation went on for about an hour, as he tried to draw out of me why I wanted to see the Commissioner.

'I'll tell you what Jock, I'll see him, make an appointment and fix it up for you. I'll see you next Tuesday at 10.00am.'

At no time during the next few days did DD speak to me. I carried out doing my work. I was not denied access to any confidential documents.

The following Tuesday I was outside Commander Jock Wilson's door.

After a few minutes his secretary came over to me.

'Mr Wilson will see you now.'

I walked into his office.

'Sit down!'

Wilson stared straight at me. No Mr Nice man now.

'I want you to listen to what I'm going to say, and listen well. I spent an hour with you last week. You tell me you want to see the Commissioner, but won't tell me why. Do you honestly think that I am going to go into the Commissioner's office and say that "a jumped-up DC wants to see you but won't tell me what it's about." Do you?'

'Well, yes, Sir, I do.'

'Well, I'm fuckin' not. You're going back to uniform at Romford, like it or not. Now get out!'

He got out of his chair, walked past me and opened the door.

'Is that it?' I asked.

'Just leave!'

A few weeks later I left New Scotland Yard, seemingly without anybody noticing.

TWENTY-FOUR
BACK TO UNIFORM

I packed my bags and reported to the uniform chief inspector at Romford Police Station. When I arrived I had long hair hanging over my shoulders. I also had sideburns, which were all part of the disguise for C11.

I walked into the Chief Inspector's office.

'So, you've come back to uniform, what's this, another bent CID reject back into uniform for us to deal with? What have you been up to?'

I looked at him.

'Bent, you don't even know the meaning of it. I've seen more bent stuff in the past few years than you could ever have dreamt about, so don't call me bent!'

And with that I turned on my heels and walked out of his office. I had only gone a few yards down the corridor when I heard his voice.

'Sorry, Jock, come back.'

I turned round and walked back to his office.

'Sir, I've never bottled a job since I joined. You've got my record. Does it read bent? I have no intention of telling you what was going on up there. Sir, all I will say it's not the job I knew on division. What I will say, however, is that I have been told to be extremely careful as there is someone out there after me and I'm likely to be stitched up.'

I went to the local hairdressers, had my head shorn and got

back into uniform for late turn shift at Romford Police Station. I was treated as a novelty. This was the first time I had been on beat duty since 1965. Romford at that time was a pretty boring place for an active copper.

On my first Sunday night on late turn, the duty sergeant decided to walk round with me on my beat.

It was somewhere around 9.00pm and in a deserted Romford High Street that the sergeant got rather excited. 'Look at all these cars.'

'Cars, what cars?' I asked.

'These ones.' He pointed out the cars on the other side of the road. 'The ones outside the cinema, they're causing an obstruction. This can be your first job, Jock, stick them all on for obstruction.'

'They're not causing any problems that I can see.'

'I'm telling you, they are causing an obstruction, so report all of them.'

'No, Sarge. You see the obstruction, I don't. You stick them on.'

He went berserk.

'Give me your pocket book.'

I undid the button on the pocket of my uniform, took out my pocket book and handed it to him.

'I'm giving you an official caution for failing to obey a lawful order.'

And with that he signed my pocketbook.

I walked off and left him. I never heard another word about it. It was becoming clear to me as to why the public were starting to turn against the police.

On 18th April, 1974, I applied to rejoin the CID. I was quite proud of my application, and after the preamble it read:

> On 16th April, 1974, I was transferred to uniform duty on K Division, serving at Romford.
>
> I have one Commissioner's Commendation for Courage and Determination leading to the arrest of a vicious criminal whereby I sustained personal injury. I was also commended at Tower Hamlets juvenile court.
>
> I have a High Commissioner's Commendation for

outstanding courage and devotion to duty in tackling three men in possession of imitation firearms and other offensive weapons.

I was also commended at Westminster Coroner's Court.

I received £20.00 from the Bow Street Reward Fund.

I have a further three Deputy Assistant Commissioner's Commendations for crime arrests.

I have had numerous arrests for criminal offences including demanding money with menaces, conspiracy to steal etc.

I was duly accepted into the CID and was posted to Romford as a Temporary Detective Constable.

A few weeks later I was at Scotland Yard and entered the Tank. As I walked over to a table to speak to some former colleagues, I felt a hand on my shoulder. I heard a voice I knew only too well.

'Where's your funny hat, son?'

I looked round; it was Dave Dilley.

'I don't have a funny hat, Guv, I am now back as a TDC.'

He drew on his Havana and looked at me.

'Oh really! That won't be for very long, we'll soon see about that.'

With that he turned and walked away with a sarcastic grin on his face.

A few days later I received a letter from the Commander of K Division, Mr P C Neivens.

It read:

'When you were posted to this position on 16th April, 1974 during an interview in my office, you stated that as a result of your impending transfer from uniform duty on Division you had requested an interview with the Commissioner, but to that date you had not received any reply beyond an interview with DAC, C (Admin). I have discussed the matter with Mr Wilson, who states that he made it quite clear that your ability to become involved in operational matters with the attendant publicity arising from your award for the India House Incident had made it necessary for you to be moved from C11. The conditions under which you were employed in C11 were that you would enjoy the status of a CID Officer as a photographer within the confines of C11. Therefore, regrettably you were to return to uniform on Division. You have now been selected for appointment as a temporary PC (CID) for duty at Romford in the near future, and I assume you do not wish to pursue your request to see the Commissioner. As you are posted night duty, I have not warned you for an interview in my office to acquaint you with the above, but should you desire to speak to me on this matter please telephone the divisional clerk.'

DD's tentacles were far-reaching, and soon I was to feel how powerful they were when I was threatened with prosecution under the Official Secrets Act.

While I had been at C11, I was involved in the arrest of dozens of people for blackmail offences. The majority of these involved sexual activities, both straight or bent. I took dozens of photographs of the blackmailers during the handover of the ransom money.

On an occasion that was to have far-reaching consequences to my life, I was asked to do a photo surveillance at Victoria railway station. This was blackmail case where a Mr 'X' was to pay £5,000 in exchange for some compromising pictures.

While we were waiting for the blackmailers to appear, Detective Sergeant Derek Ramsay, disguised as a vicar, walked onto the station concourse carrying a Bible under his arm. He sat down on one of the station benches and smiled at the elderly woman sitting next to him. She acknowledged him with a shy smile. Ramsay opened his Bible and made a pretence of reading it. After a few minutes, they were joined by a down-and-out carrying his worldly possessions. He entered into conversation with the 'vicar', but suddenly picked up his things and quickly shuffled away, immediately followed by the elderly lady. Her face was screwed-up, and she was shaking her head. Almost immediately afterwards, a man and woman approached the victim as he stood at a pre-arranged position near to Ramsay.

The three of them had a short conversation and two packages were exchanged. Ramsay and a further ten plainclothes officers, who beforehand had been mingling in the crowd, rushed forward to arrest the two.

As they culprits were being led away, I asked Ramsay what had happened on the bench.

'What?' Ramsay asked.

'The old bum and the woman on the bench.'

'Oh, the dirty old git tried to tap me up for a couple of bob and I told him to fuck off.'

'Cheers, vicar,' I said.

As the female was put into a waiting police car, I took a personal photograph of her with my Pentax camera. At a later date I processed the negative at home.

Both of the accused subsequently appeared at the Old Bailey charged with blackmail. They pleaded guilty, and the female was sentenced to twelve months' imprisonment, suspended for two years. Her boyfriend, a private investigator, was sentenced to two years' imprisonment.

It was revealed at the trial that Mr X, a wealthy City tycoon and a figure in local politics, had been having sexual encounters with his secretary. She, along with her boyfriend, concocted the blackmail plot after Mr X had called her into his office one day. When she entered he was as naked as the day he was born and holding his collection of whips and bondage equipment. He then asked her to tie him up and lock him in his cupboard, a request that I am sure many secretaries would have willing obliged and then thrown away the key. The blackmailers subsequently set up a hidden camera to capture the festivities when his secretary obliged him in the future.

I took my photo to the *News of the World* and they duly published it. I was aware that taking personal photographs on duty was against regulations, and that selling them to the media would certainly provoke disciplinary action. This was a wrong decision on my part, and was something I had never considered doing before. However, in my anger and frustration over the destruction of my career, I believed I would then have had the opportunity to expose before a disciplinary board the issues I had hoped to speak to the Commissioner about.

A few days after the publication of the photograph I was called into the office of the local detective inspector.

'You're going to be interviewed tomorrow at 2.00pm by a Detective Chief Inspector Batchelor and some others from the Yard. What the hell is going on, Jim?'

'I haven't a clue, Guv'nor. I'll see them tomorrow.'

TWENTY-SIX

THE BEGINNING OF THE END

I watched as the detective sergeant started to write my statement.

'James Smith, Eleven, Six, Forty-one...'

I paused.

'Okay, I've got that, now are you going to do this statement or not?' Batchelor asked.

The detective sergeant stared at me. I didn't say anything.

'Well, while you're sitting there thinking, let me refresh your memory. You were at the *News of the World* offices this morning. We also know that a week ago you took a blonde tasty-looking bird, a reporter from that very paper, and showed her the indices in C11. You refused to tell the officers on the desk who she was. Correct?'

'Can you prove I was at the newspaper office this morning?'

'You prove you were elsewhere and I'll listen.'

'I was in South London.'

'Prove it.'

'OK, I had myself photographed for approximately two hours where I was.'

'You had yourself photographed? That doesn't sound like the actions of an innocent man to me.'

'Guv'nor, can I have a glass of water?'

'When we are ready.'

'No, now please.'

'Mouth drying up is it, finding it difficult to talk? It's the nerves. It'll be better when you get things off your chest.'

'No, I am suffering from kidney stones and I have to drink constantly.'

'In a minute, Jim; this will soon be over. A quick statement and then you can go.'

'And if I refuse?'

'You will be disobeying a lawful order.'

'I require a glass of water.'

'Get him some water.'

The DC left the room. There was silence until he returned.

I drank it down in a 'one-er'.

'Better now, Jock?'

'Yes, thanks, but I'll need a pee soon.'

He looked at me, raised his voice and said, 'Don't mess me about!'

'I'm not, but tell me what you've got and I'll tell you what I've got, and I'll make a statement under caution, fair enough?'

'Yes, OK. You went on a Friday night at about 7.00pm to the C11 office. You had a blonde with you. She was a bit of a stunner. You knew the two officers at the desk. You refused to tell them who she was. You took an envelope from C11 and inside the envelope were the negatives of this picture. You then left and went to the *News of the World* with her, and that's it. Jim, you're captured. It's hands-up time.'

'OK, one pee and then I'll fill you in.'

'Take him to the toilet.'

With that, a DC walked me to the toilet and watched me pee.

As we re-entered the interview room there was an abrupt end to the conversation in progress.

'Better Jock?'

'Yes, thanks.'

Batchelor looked at me.

'OK, in your own words, Jock, let's get this cleared up and then, as I said, we can all go home. Where would you like to start?'

'I have been a victim of persecution by a Commander, David Dilley. I believe that he is aware that I have information of corruption relating to him and other officers.'

'Stop right there!'

He looked over to the other officers.

'Don't write anything yet, don't write anything. We are not here to discuss Mr Dilley. We are here because you stole photographs from C11.'

'Well, I bet you were sent here by Dave Dilley, am I correct?'

'I am not here to investigate anything other than your actions.'

'Well, I'm telling you he is out to get me, hook, line and sinker.'

'OK, let's go back to the statement.'

'What's he got on you, Guv, are you frightened of him? 'cause believe me I'm not, I've had enough. Let's get on with the statement. OK, on Friday last I went to CO, C11. I was in company with a blonde female, as you state. She was dressed in jeans and a white top. I entered the C11 office and signed in.'

The officer was writing furiously.

Batchelor interrupted.

'Jim, for the purpose of the statement what was her name and occupation?'

'Yes, can I leave that to the end, Guv'nor?'

Eyebrows were raised and he screwed his mouth slightly.

'Yes, fair enough, Jock, but don't be messing us about, we know all about the *News of the World* staff.'

I continued.

'The female did not pass the desk into C11. The two officers on duty asked her who she was, and before she could answer I jokingly said, 'Don't tell them, they're dirty old men.' It was said flippantly, and we all laughed. I pointed out the general layout of the office and we passed the time of day. I collected the envelope and we left.'

'Eh, just one thing, Jim, we have examined the Visitor's Book at the reception desk into Scotland Yard. You didn't book her in. Why? You are aware all visitors must be booked in. Did you take her through the car park?'

'No, Sir, just like me she produced her warrant card and we walked through.'

I thought Batchelor was going to take off!

'Warrant card, what fucking warrant card?'

'Her warrant card, sir, she was no more from the *News of the World* than fly in the air. She is a WPC working at this station. We were both doing a drug job under the supervision of a 'straight' detective sergeant, and in fact he wrote in the Duty Book, 'Jim, don't forget to go to CO and collect the photos.' You see, Sir, the envelope - the envelope that you say contained negatives stolen from C11 - contained CRO (Criminal Records Office) pictures which had been printed for us to use in identifying pushers in Romford.'

They all looked at each other in disbelief.

'Go and get the Duty Book,' Batchelor ordered, and with that the DC left.

We in the room remained silent. After a few minutes, the DC returned and put the Duty Book in front of Batchelor. He opened it and looked at the page. The detective sergeant's entry was there.

All three studied the book, and then Batchelor stood up, turned his back on me and walked across the room, then stared out of the window for a couple of minutes before turning round and re-examining the page. He put the book back on the table, shook his head then turned to one of his officers.

'Go and get that Skipper and ask him what's going on.'

The DC left and once more silence returned to the room.

After about 10 minutes the DC returned and handed Mr Batchelor a note. He read it, studied it again and turned to the DC and said, 'Go and get the Plonk', referring to the WPC.

'I have done,' the detective sergeant replied.

'Well, what?' Batchelor asked.

'It was her, Guv'nor.'

'What do you mean it was her?'

'It was her who went with him to CO that day.'

Silence again returned to the room. Batchelor walked up and down in deep thought. The other two sat staring at the floor.

'Have you got anything at home that belongs to the

Commissioner?' Batchelor asked.

I thought for a minute.

'I have uniforms, torches, a truncheon, handcuffs… oh, no, the handcuffs are mine, I bought them privately when I was on the SPG.'

'Not those things, any other photos?'

'I have a photograph of the three who killed the Guv'nor in Blackpool. I use it for lectures. It's mounted on a piece of boarding.'

I didn't think they were really listening to me.

'That's from the job that Dilley knew all about.'

Mr Batchelor nodded to one of the DCs, and they left me in the room in company of an officer. After a few minutes they returned.

'OK, Jock, we are going now. We will be in touch.'

They put their papers into a briefcase.

Whilst they were standing up and I was sat at the desk, I looked at them.

'There's at least one bent Commander up at CO. I've been offered three grand by a DS to alter my evidence, and you're here to investigate me over a poxy photograph, no doubt sent by the very man who once described you to me as 'a tricky bastard' when you asked for my assistance in the murder enquiry at Tower Bridge. What about the statement, do you want me to sign it?'

'No, that won't be necessary,' Batchelor said.

'Oh, and by the way, Guv'nor, I was not lying about having my picture taken over a period of two hours this morning. As you said, 'not the actions of an innocent man'. Well, Sir, I am innocent and the pictures were taken at St Thomas's Hospital. They were X-rays and I was having iodine pumped into me while I was strapped to a revolving bench. The appointment for this was made some two to three weeks ago. Here is my appointment card.'

I took the card from my pocket and put it on the table.

With that Batchelor shook his head and walked off.

I was devastated. I had expected discipline, but not an attempt to fit me up under the Official Secrets Act. This had gone too far.

Inspector Woodland's words rang in my ears: 'Be careful, Jim, he'll try and fit you up'.

By giving the picture to a newspaper I had inadvertently played into the bent senior officers' hands.

I just knew 'The Old Rascal', as Dilley was known by officers who served with him, was behind it.

I returned home, and two days later I had collapsed with an attack of kidney stones and was rushed to St Thomas's Hospital by ambulance. I was pumped full of pethidine, and due to the fact there were no beds available I was sent home. I was certified sick for two weeks and within a few days was back in St Thomas's having a stone removed. This entailed removing a rib, and I still to this day carry the thirteen-inch scar on my left hand side. I was off sick for months.

Eventually I received a letter instructing me to attend the Chief Medical Officer at Tintagel House on the south bank of the Thames, next to what is now the new MI5 building.

I entered the room, where I saw the CMO sitting behind his desk. He had a one-page report in front of him.

'Come in, sit down,' he said. 'I have a report here stating that you have been off sick for many weeks now. This is a considerable amount of time, and the person reporting this to me is suggesting you are malingering.'

'Sir, I would suggest that that report was sent to you by Commander David Dilley.'

'Well, as a matter of fact, it was. Does that make a difference?'

'Well, yes, I am not malingering, and he is no longer my Commander, so why should he be interested in me?'

'Well, you tell me what is wrong with you, I don't have your case papers in front of me.'

'Sir, I have been in St Thomas's and had a large kidney stone removed.'

'What, ah...'

He said a word which I did not really understand.

I looked at him and said, 'If that's removing a rib and taking a stone out, that's what I had.'

He smiled.

'Do you have your hospital number with you?'

'Yes, Sir, here it is.'

With that he picked up the phone and relayed it to someone at the end. Within a few minutes his secretary entered the room and handed him a note. He read it and stood up. A friendlier atmosphere was now in the room.

'OK, jacket off, on to the bench.'

I climbed onto the bench.

'Pull up your shirt.'

I pulled up my shirt.

'Ah, yes, I see.'

He gently touched the wound.

'That's healing up nicely. Come back in one hour.'

One hour later I was back.

'OK, I've got your records,' the CMO said. 'You've been through the wars. Well, I'm happy you're not malingering. You seem concerned by this.'

'Well, yes, Sir, I am, but I don't want to go into it all. But the man that signed that - David Dilley - well, let's say he wants me done. I've done nothing except possibly spoken out of place about his erm, eh… let's say misconduct.'

I felt myself welling up.

With that the CMO looked up and closed my file.

'OK, just take it easy. I see you went back in uniform. Do you feel confident to go back on street duty and get involved in fights and all the things you chaps get involved in?'

'I'm actually back out as a TDC.'

'Back in the CID?'

'Yes, Sir, I do, but I think, feel, that things are being made so difficult that I will resign. I am not going out on a 'sickie'.'

He looked over his glasses.

'I am putting you off on sick leave for the next two months. Now go home, relax and take things easy. You've had major surgery. No interviews and no police work, and think seriously about what I said.'

'Thank you, Sir.'

I walked to the door, and as I did so I heard his voice again.

'Think seriously about your ability to carry on as a serving police officer after having this operation. I will be thinking about it,' he smiled.

I felt at least that one person was on my side.

Nothing much happened over the next few weeks and eventually it came to the time for me to attend Buckingham Palace to receive my BEM from the Queen. I had no enquiries regarding my health from any police officer. I had no offer of a car to take me and my family to Buckingham Palace which was normal practice.

A few days after the Investiture I received a call from a member of Batchelor's team.

'You will be required to attend an Identification Parade at Romford Police Station next Tuesday at 2.00pm.'

This identification parade would have been held to identify the person who brought the photograph into the *News of the World* office.

'Hang on a minute, I am not going on any parade. Have you seen the CMO report - 'no interviews'? And besides, my pictures have been all over the national press. And not only that, I have a report signed by Peter Neivens agreeing with Dilley and his lapdog Wilson that my career has been blown because of publicity. How can I get a fair ID parade? Oh, and by the way, ask Dave Dilley why another decorated officer is still working at C11... he's been in all the Nationals and he's still there. No, I'm sorry, I won't be there. If you want to nick me, please be gentle, I'm off sick. Goodbye.'

I never heard another thing.

On 30th January, 1975, I resigned from the police. It was the hardest thing I had to do in all my service. The police was like a family to me - I felt very close to cops. A number of fellow officers tried to persuade me to stay.

On my resignation paper I wrote in the space allocated to Reason for Leaving:

'Tried to see Commissioner re: corruption... refused.'

I thought that even at this late stage I might get a hearing. I didn't. I went downstairs with my uniform to hand it to the store man. As I did so, he looked at me and put his hands out towards me.

'Whoa, whoa, hold on a minute, I can't take that.'

'Why?'

'You're suspended.'

'Suspended? Here have a look at this.' I showed him my warrant card. 'If you're suspended that goes, right? I'm not suspended, so take the uniform.'

'Oh, oh, I'm sorry, I heard a rumour.'

'Don't listen to rumours, they're seldom true. I heard another one the other day that you're a poof. Is that true?'

I walked out.

Back upstairs, I took out my warrant card and wrote across it, 'Cancelled'. In the pit of my stomach I felt sick. I handed it to the detective inspector.

'I think I know what this is.'

He took it and read it.

'I was supposed to cancel it.'

'I saved you a job, Guv'nor. Anything else?'

'No, good luck. Keep your head down.'

I left the nick with some 'real policemen', and we went for a coffee at the Wimpy Bar at Romford market. That was my farewell do. I felt naked without my warrant card, and that my life had been taken from me.

I was in a daze as I drove home. I was no longer a police office, after all the time counting the years until I was old enough to join. I felt hurt, near to tears. There was no person I could go to. How I hated these handful of bent senior officers at the Yard who had ruined my career and my life.

I arrived home and walked up our small driveway. My wife was standing at the window crying, she had been through the hell of this with me. My two boys were sitting on the sofa, wondering what was going on. I opened the door and walked into the house. My wife came over to me.

'They let you out?'

'Out? What do you mean out?' I asked.

'They didn't keep you in?'

'In?'

'Yes, I've just had a phone call from Mr Davis at Romford Police Station telling me that you had been arrested and would not be home.'

I went straight to the phone and dialled Romford nick.

'Mr Davis, please.'

'Davis speaking.'

'Jim Smith here, you just phoned my wife and told her that I was banged up. Is that correct?'

'Yes.'

'Why?'

'Well, that's what I was told.'

'By who?'

'I can't say. It came from above.'

'A rumour?'

'Uh, uh…'

'By who? Who? I'll have your bollocks if you phone my wife again. And while you're at it, phone David Dilley and tell him that the next time I speak to him will be at Number One Court at the Old Bailey.'

'But I…'

I hung up. We didn't sleep much that night, after I counted the minutes to midnight when my Police career ended.

Jim Smith (far right)
at Hendon Training School, 1962

Commandant Tommy Wall

Ali Salih Hussein, the man who tried to kill
Jim and shot two police officers two days later

Jim Smith, SPG, in 1966

Breakfast in Anguilla. L-R: George Burrows, BEM (left with coffee mug); Dick Pearce (centre with sungalsses); Gordon Grier (seated facing camera); Yours truly.

New supplies and extra officers arrive in Anguilla

Shower time in Anguilla

"Jungle clearing" in Anguilla

Jim in disguise, Soho, early 1960s

Nick 'Birchie' Birch

DI Bob Watt, the man in charge of
the investigation of Mrs Roberts

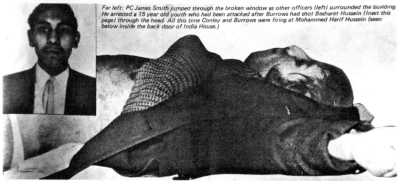

Far left: PC James Smith jumped through the broken window as other officers (left) surrounded the building. He arrested a 15 year old youth who had been attacked after Burrows had shot Basharet Hussein (Inset this page) through the head. All this time Conley and Burrows were firing at Mohammed Harif Hussein (seen below inside the back door of India House.)

Jim with his parents, Janet and Gregory at Buckingham Palace

C11 Office, New Scotland Yard, 1970

TOP YARD MEN IN QUIZ OVER RICH FRIENDS

By TREVOR KEMPSON

AN investigation has been launched into links between some ex-members of Scotland Yard's Criminal Intelligence Department—C11—and several top English and international financiers.

The probe is being carried out by the Yard's A10 branch, which investigates allegations of internal corruption.

Sir Eric Miller, deposed boss of the £40 million Peachey property empire, is believed to be among those to be asked to help the probe team.

They will also want to interview Judah Binstock—known as the "Mr Big" of international currency deals.

One of Binstock's closest associates since he left England has been former Detective Sergeant Mike Franklin, who was in C11 for a considerable time. He resigned in 1969.

Promoted

The A10 investigators will also see a serving policeman, Detective Chief Superintendent John Groves. He was promoted recently when he left C11.

A third man who will be helping the inquiry is ex-Commander David Dilley, who left the force last August. He was head of C11 for six years.

Mr Dilley has made a statement to A10, but he said: "In no way do police inquiries affect me."

He added: "As far as I'm aware, I've never met Judah Binstock in my life. But I do know of him."

DILLEY: "The police inquiries don't affect me"

Above: Mr Dilley gives a present

Left: *News of The World*, 5th June 1977: Dilley denies all

The only photographs of the missing Joseph and Michael Debono held by their mother

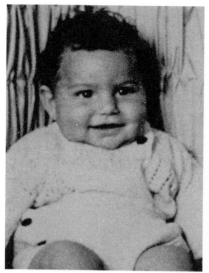

Jim finds the boys in Malta, and reunites them with their mother

Bringing the missing children back from Spain

Reunited with Grandad Bob

Jim with Pedro in Fuengirola Police Station, Costa del Sol

Winton, Joelle and Janet in the Mijas Hotel, Costa del Sol

Gregory, Janet, Steven and Jim on Gregiry's wedding day

Reunited and exchanging gifts with Pedro, thirty years later

TWENTY-SEVEN
CIVVY STREET

It was two weeks after leaving the police force that I was due to start my new job with a small security company in the City of London. I was to be the assistant security operations manager. The company had some very good contracts with blue chip companies, and were involved with the escorting of high value works of art.

Five days before I was due to start, I received a phone call from Dick Berry, the owner of the company.

'Jim, could you please come in and see us ASAP?' he asked.

'Yes, I'll come in this afternoon.'

There was a note of hard concern in his voice.

Later that day at the company's office in Britton Street, he said: 'Jim, I'll come straight to the point. We have made some unofficial checks on you with the police. Our source has not been too kind to you, his exact words were, "My man says don't take him, he's bent".'

'Bent! Bent! Dick, I want the name of the man because I'll sue him.'

'What's it all about, Jim?'

'I have never done a bent thing in my life. Go back to your man and ask him if it came from Dave Dilley, the Commander at the Yard.'

'Jim, listen, we are still going to start you, but be aware there are people out there gunning for you.'

Perhaps I was getting paranoid, but I was convinced I was being followed. My wife and I were receiving phone calls during the night, with heavy breathing on the line. No voices, just heavy breathing, and then the line would go silent. I was convinced that our phone had been 'hooked up'. I was using telephone boxes for calls.

The warrants for telephone intercepts had to be approved by the Home Secretary, but in most cases these were rubber-stamped. If Dilley had wanted to have my line 'hooked up' he would have a solid gold reason - the Official Secrets Act. After all, if he could hook up Lester Piggott, years before his tax troubles, in order to get racing tips, then he'd have no trouble hooking up me.

I had a contact at a national newspaper - not the *News of the World*. When I went to see him, he agreed to assist me with a plan I had put together.

It was quite simple.

At a given time, I telephoned the newspaper from home and asked for the contact.

He answered, 'Hi, Jim, how's things?'

'OK, did you get the picture?'

'Yes, what is it?'

'It's the top table at the C11 stag night.'

'Got you, I'm looking at the faces as I am talking to you. That's Bernie Silver, isn't it?'

'Yes.'

'Who's that guy sitting next to him?'

'Which one?'

'The big guy.'

'That's Dave Dilley, the man I talked to you about, the head of the Criminal Intelligence Department.'

'What, Silver's there as a guest of a Commander of the Met?'

'Spot on... If I get any more grief, I'll give you a signed declaration or whatever you want to publish this picture. I am at my wits' end.'

'So, we've got one of the top Commanders, and some would say the most powerful, sitting at the top table with his guest Bernie

Silver, the country's biggest 'porno man', who Dilley's invited to the Criminal Intelligence stag night?'

My contact was 'carrying the plot', as it's said.

'Correct,' I replied.

'Who's the thinner guy down from him?'

'That's Frederick James Pickles, who runs the Intercept Office. His nickname is 'Wilf' Pickles, after the old guy who was on the radio years ago whose catch phrase was "Give 'em the money Barney!" In the case of the guy in the picture, it was "take the money!"'

'Holy shit, are they all at it?'

'Well, it looks that way, but not all of them, only this crowd at the top.'

'Never mind your problems, this picture could open up a can of worms, this is hot stuff.'

Along with at least one hundred officers, I had witnessed the scene as described. However, there was no picture. I was banking that Dilley and company would be very worried indeed if a photographic record of this indiscretion existed.

A few days later I received a call at work from my 'Investigating Officer'.

'Hi, Jim, I have been instructed to inform you that no further action will be brought regarding the *News of the World* photograph.'

I answered sarcastically, 'Oh Cheers... thanks very much!'

'It must have been a difficult time for you?'

'Who gave you this number?'

'Erm, I'm not sure... it was just left on my desk with a message. If you want to collect the negatives that we took from your desk at Romford, they will be in my office.'

'No thanks, you deliver them to my home address.'

They duly arrived. They were holiday negatives of my wife and kids; there were no kidnap negatives. The whole incident finally drew to a close. Certain senior officers had achieved the results they had wanted - me out of the police. Despite my best intentions, I had assisted them by giving that picture to the *News of the World*. I wish I hadn't, but one thing is for sure, I didn't steal anything.

The next three years brought about remarkable changes in Scotland Yard. The exposure of corruption there shocked the public and became a national scandal.

'Wally' Virgo was convicted of corruption at the Old Bailey.

Ken Drury was convicted of corruption at the Old Bailey.

'Jock' Wilson was transferred to the Traffic Department.

David Clarence Dilley retired and died a few years later.

I remained with the security company for about six months, when I was then offered consultancy work with a number of hotels in London. At this particular time the IRA was in full flow, and was bombing premises in central London.

One of the companies I was working for was the Selfridge Hotel owned by EMI. The hotel was situated behind the famous Selfridges store, and amongst my instructions I was to investigate thefts and introduce bomb evacuation procedures.

While working there I was asked to do various tasks and, as a result of my enquiries, the Chief Accountant was arrested and charged with theft. Their chief security officer resigned after I discovered that he was stealing property from the lost property store. It was during this period that I noticed the man working in the gift shop was none other than the 'gunrunner' whom I had photographed some years previously at the Cumberland Hotel.

I started to befriend him. I was 100% certain that this was the man. I telephoned the Criminal Intelligence Department at Scotland Yard and spoke to one of the officers. I had known this officer for some time, but was never completely impressed by his ability. However, he reluctantly came to see me. I explained the situation to him and pointed out the man. I referred to my photographs at C11, giving him the dates to within a month that I had taken them. He left the hotel and I never heard from him again.

A few weeks after his visit I was approached by a female member of staff at the hotel; I will call her 'Gill'. She was in a very distressed state. After a while, I calmed her down and she then told me the most remarkable story.

'Mr Smith, I am being blackmailed by a man working in the hotel. He has discovered something about my past and he is threatening to reveal it. I could be in serious trouble.'

'How much money have you paid him?'

'No, no, it is not money. He is making me do things which could get me into trouble.'

'What type of things?'

'He's getting me to send telex messages to people abroad from the hotel, and then gets me to hide the replies and give them to him at a later time. I'm scared stiff. When telephone calls come in for him he gets them transferred to the house on the first floor at the far end of the lounge, and he makes out that he staying in the hotel.'

'Well, that's not going to give you too much trouble. What's on the telexes?'

'Mr Smith, I'm scared to tell you. Honestly, this is really scary and serious stuff.'

'I can't help you if you don't tell me.'

'Can I trust you?'

'Yes, honestly you can.'

'OK, I'll tell you. He is supplying guns to people.'

'Supplying guns?'

'Yes, he's gun-running.'

'Who is this person?'

'It's George Vassiliou, the man who works in the gift shop. Please, please don't tell anyone.'

About two weeks later, Gill telephoned me.

'Can we meet, I have something to show you?'

'OK, where would you like to meet?'

'Anywhere but the hotel, I'm scared stiff that he will discover what I am doing.'

'OK, how about the Italian café in North Audley Street. It's just next to the gent's outfitters. Do you know it?'

'Yes, I think I've been there, I'll see you about 1.30 if that's OK.'

'OK, that's OK with me. I'll see you then, bye.'

I arrived at the café ten minutes early. I ordered a cappuccino. After a few minutes Gill arrived and came over and sat next to me.

'I don't know if I want to go through with this. Now, can I honestly trust you?'

'Yes, but the ball's in your court. I will not breathe a word of it to anyone within the hotel, and I will never disclose your name to anyone.'

'I'm worried if he…'

'Well, you either trust me or you don't.'

With that she handed me a copy of the *London Evening Standard*.

'Read the paper inside at page 3.'

My immediate reaction was that she may have been watching too many James Bond films.

I opened the paper, and inside there was an A4 page with typing on it. I started to read it.

It read:

Attention Doctor Giuid Castro.

And then there was a telephone number in Lisbon.
The first line read:

2,000 M16 US $260 each.

The next line read:

40 M rounds US $160 per 1,000.

Next line read…

10,000 G3 US $210 each.

All FOB Europe plus commission.

Contact Mr Silva Leal.

There then followed a list of telephone numbers, and finally it read, 'Awaiting your quick report back.'

I looked at it and raised my eyebrows a little, but I could not let Gill know that this was the man who I had photographed some years earlier.

'Can I keep this?'

'Yes, but don't take it into the hotel. Please Jim - you don't mind

'Oh, yes, he has property in Norfolk, a large farm, and his references from other banks are very, very good.'

'If this thing is kosher, how come the other banks are not biting his hand off for the business?' I asked.

'They're only high street branches. He's come to us because of our background, and of course, our bank being Irish and we are in the bloodstock business.'

'So, you're telling me that your bank wants to plough thousands of pounds into this guy?'

'Jim, millions, it's millions,' he replied.

I just about choked on my coffee.

'Shergar, IRA, millions of pounds. This sounds, to say the least, a bit iffy.'

'No, Jim, it could be a tremendous business investment for us.'

'This client of yours, do you know who he is working for?'

'Ah, yes. Now this is top secret; there are only the head people in the Bank who are aware of this.'

We sat in silence in the empty room as he looked from side to side, up and down, as if he was expecting to find some spy hiding behind the curtains. It had all the atmosphere of Inspector Clouseau.

After a pregnant pause, he whispered, 'It's the Sultan of Brunei.'

'Sorry?'

'Yes, Jim, the Sultan of Brunei.'

'Well, the Sultan's got a few quid, how come he's not putting in a few bob himself?' I asked.

'Ah, well, as I say, it's a bit complicated.'

'Complicated?'

I waited for his reply.

'Can you find out if he has got a criminal record? You know what I mean, through your old pals.'

He gently tapped the side of his nose with his index finger.

'I presume you mean your client, and not the Sultan.'

'Yes, exactly, Jim.'

Give me his details and I'll check him out by other means. The days of being able to check out people for convictions are over, it's strictly illegal.'

'OK. His name is Kersey, he's a really nice guy. Oh, by the way, we don't have a big budget on this.'

'Hang on a minute… you're going to give him five, ten, twenty million for Shergar's foal, and you don't have a big budget for me to check him out?'

'Well, shall we say, five hundred pounds?'

'Go on, say it,' I replied.

'Ah, Jaesus, you're an awful man. Five hundred pounds for the initial enquiry and another five hundred or so if you can prove he's got a criminal record. Now, how does that grab you?'

'OK, it's a start. You put five hundred pounds on account into my bank account, OK?'

'We would like you to start at once,' he said.

'How long will it take for your money to clear into my account?'

'Five days,' he replied.

'OK, then that's when I'll start, in five days' time.'

I was loving it.

'Oh, well, under the circumstances, I am sure we could credit your account instantly.'

And with that, he handed me his client's details.

'Such a nice guy.' I remembered the words of Sid Hall, a detective sergeant who played a leading part in the conviction of the Kray twins: 'You will never meet a conman who wasn't liked by his victim. It's part of his trade.'

I left the bank and made some enquiries on Mr Kersey, having assumed that this was his correct name. I was convinced that he was a criminal but how to prove this, as there was no way to view his criminal records?

I checked out his address at Duckfoot Farm, Bush Green, Diss in Norfolk. It checked out OK. He was living at that address.

He claimed to have been in banking and to have served with the RAF police. He said he had broken his neck on two occasions and had spent some time in hospital. I telephoned the Special Branch at Norfolk Police and explained the situation. As expected, they were not prepared to discuss the matter with me.

'You see, Sir, we can't give you any information. You tell me you are a private investigator. I don't know you from Adam and, by the way, where did you get this number from?'

'Directory Enquires gave me your Headquarters number, I dialled it and when the woman answered I asked for SB and was put through. It was as simple as that! Now do you want the information or not?'

'Yes, we will take it, but we will be unable to confirm or deny anything.'

I told them what I had, and in particular the alleged IRA connection. I gave them my details, and as far as I was concerned that was the end the matter with them.

A few days later, I received a phone call from Chief Superintendent Bunn of Norwich police.

'I understand that you have been trying to get some information from our Special Branch regarding some chap?'

'I'm sorry, I'm not looking for information. I was trying to give it to them. But as usual with SB, they are so full of their own importance they couldn't detect a pickled onion in a fruit salad.'

He chuckled. I told him the story.

'Interesting, you say there's an IRA connection?' he asked.

'No, Kersey does. My own feeling is that it is one big con.'

'Well, thank you very much for that. As you will appreciate, we can't discuss the matter with you,' he said, and then rang off.

I searched the British Newspaper Library records at Colindale in North London for any mention of Peter Neville Kersey, but I couldn't find anything. Oh well, in for a penny, in for a pound, I thought. Why not give Kersey a call, what have I got to lose?

I connected my tape recorder and rang the farm. After a few seconds the phone was answered.

'Hello,' a male voice said.

'Mr Kersey, please.' I said.

'Speaking.'

'Ah, Tom McDonald at relations here, aftercare service,' I said. 'I don't believe we have met, and for the life of me I can't understand why your file has arrived on my desk in Glasgow.'

'Glasgow? There must be some mistake. I've never been in trouble in Scotland,' he said.

'Eh, that is Mr Kersey?'

'Yes, yes, but no, no, not in Scotland.'

'Well, why on earth have I got your file?' I asked.

'I can't help you, what does it say Mr McDonald?'

'Well, you know the system, Peter; you don't mind if I call you Peter?

'No, no,' he replied.

I can't tell you what it says.'

'Yes, yes, I understand.'

'Well, anyway, how are you?' I asked.

'I'm very well, thank you.'

'Settling in OK?'

'Yes, fine.'

'Now, from what I can see, you have never been in trouble where violence has been involved.'

'Oh, no, Sir, I abhor violence.'

'How would you describe your life with regards to the effect of the custodial sentences you have had?'

He then went on to describe his life of crime, one con after the other, and then the details of his custodial sentences. He wouldn't stop talking.

'Well, Peter, thank you very much for all your help, and kind regards to your good lady. I will note your comments on your file and I'll pass it on to our Norwich office as soon as possible, and trust they will not trouble you for some time. I understand we will all be computerized in the near future and this will do away with these problems.'

'Thank you, Sir, that is very kind of you, and thank you for your continuing interest in me.'

'No trouble, Peter. Goodbye, or as we say up here in Glasgow, "awe ra best."'

I replaced the handset in my office in Berkshire and saluted the conman with two fingers! Oh, to con a conman!

I arranged a meeting with the bank for the next day, where I was introduced to three senior bank officials sitting round the boardroom table.

'Gentlemen,' I said, 'as I explained to David here, it is a criminal offence to obtain copies of criminal records. However, I have done my best and have Mr Kersey's criminal past recorded on this tape. As you will hear, it comes direct from the horse's mouth, if you'll excuse the pun.'

They sat in silence and listened as the tape played.

When the tape stopped, David burst out, 'Jaesus almighty, the lying bastard. And here I was thinking I was going to make a few Punts on his wee horse. Oh, Jaesus, and he was such a nice man.'

I asked if the bank wished to take the matter any further, but this was declined.

Eventually, after two reminders, I received my fees, and as far as I was concerned that was the end of the matter. However, a few months later I received a phone call from the CID at Norwich:

'You may remember you spoke to my boss, regarding this chap Kersey.'

'Yes, what can I do for you?'

'Well, he's been arrested and I was wondering if there is any further information you may have.'

'No, I'm sorry, I gave your Guv'nor everything I had,' I said.

'Well, Kersey's been charged here with fraud. In less than two years he has had banks 'over' in excess of half a million pounds to finance his lifestyle. He's managed to get hold of one of the Queen's flights… oh, it's a long story. Anyway, if there is nothing you can add to yours, I'll leave you now. Goodbye.'

'Just a minute, did all this take place after I supplied your force with the information?' I asked.

'Yes, I suppose it must have, now you mention it,' he said.

This kind of thing is enough to make one weep. The police are spoonfed and still manage to die of starvation. Since they didn't take a blind bit of notice about the information I supplied, I guess I wasn't under consideration for a reward!

Kersey appeared at Norwich Crown Court, where his story was unfolded in detail. Between April 1986 and February 1988, he posed as a representative of the oil-rich Sultan of Brunei and had ordered aircraft valued at £120 million. I can only guess that the foal story hadn't worked out. By using false letters and documents, he conned various bank managers into lending him hundreds of thousands of pounds while he embarked on extravagant trips. He even offered an honest Norwich businessman a chief executive's job with an annual salary of £83,000. In all, he conned High Street banks out of £600,000 in less than two years.

His biggest con was when he tricked the RAF into lending him one of the Queen's £20 million private jets for a flight in Norfolk. British Aerospace swallowed his story hook, line and sinker; believing him to be a potential buyer, as Mr Kersey claimed to be setting up an airline. They were so impressed by the future 'airline chief' that a lounge at Norwich airport was refurbished for the arrival of Mr Kersey, the 'personal representative of the Sultan of Brunei'. After all, he was arriving in the Queen's flight, who wouldn't believe him.

Word soon got to the Sultan, who was not impressed. Diplomatic sources made enquiries with Norwich police and up popped the name 'Kersey'.

In November 1988 he was sentenced to three years' imprisonment at Norwich Crown Court.

After his release, he was back in Norfolk where he set up in business in a luxury office suite at the Hethersett Business Centre. This time he was running the bogus Cranberry Trust for the disabled. To add credence to the charity, he conned the Princess of Wales' staff into sending him best wishes for his project. The letter was proudly displayed on his office wall.

He then went on to represent a US Foundation, who he said wanted to donate £6 million to charity. This time, James Ruddy of the *Eastern Daily Press* exposed him and the con failed.

And Shergar? He was never found. He's now folk history in Irish bars.

TWENTY-NINE
DO YOU DO MATRIMONIAL WORK?

During my years as a private investigator I was frequently asked if I would undertake matrimonial work. I did investigate a few cases, but to be honest I always did so reluctantly, and usually only to keep the wolf from the door. This type of work is always the seedier side of investigation, and has involved me in the past in such activities as filming a vicar having a sex session with a female parishioner two minutes after his wife had left the Manse! But, sometimes, one thing leads to another.

One evening I received a telephone call at home from a colleague.

'I'm over in Paris at the moment,' he said, 'two of us are doing a job for an American multi-millionaire. They're staying in one of Paris's top hotels and the client is concerned about his and his wife's safety, particularly with regard to kidnapping, as they have had some threatening telephone calls. I am going to need your services. Can you make your way north tomorrow toward Braemar, approximately six miles from Balmoral Castle, where the client has a property where the client's wife will be in couple of days?'

As part of the Paris-side of the operation, it had been agreed to run an intercept on the telephone in the hotel suite of the client and his wife. In the event of any more threatening calls being made, these would be recorded and could be used as evidence. The husband did not wish his wife to be aware of the tap, as he was afraid that it would cause her unnecessary upset and worry.

After setting up an intercept matters had proceeded uneventfully, until one evening when the client's wife excused herself during dinner with her husband in the hotel restaurant to return to the suite to 'powder her nose'. Whilst in the room she made a telephone call to a man the USA.

Later that night my colleagues listened to her conversation and there was no doubt that the two of them had been having 'telephone sex'. In a steamy cloud of suggestive talk the man described, as he slapped his penis on his office desk, just how he would like to further employ his member.

Experienced private investigators are rarely shocked, but my colleagues were amazed that such an attractive and well-looked-after woman would take part in such lewd activity over a trans-Atlantic telephone line.

A decision had to be made; should they tell her husband? Although the conversation wasn't precisely a threat to him, they decided that he should know. The following morning, while the wife was out shopping, the client was told of the call. He was initially disbelieving and then insisted on listening to the tape. Despite my colleagues' suggestion that this was perhaps unwise, he demanded to hear it. He sat in deep silence as the tape was replayed, with tears running down his face.

"Have you any idea who the man is?" he was asked.

"Oh, yes, I know who he is. He is one of our Governors in the States and I have been financing his campaign. That funding stops now and I want all the evidence you can get."

Meanwhile, I had travelled up to Scotland and as instructed kept the cottage where was she was staying under observation. Their nearby mansion was in the process of a multi-million pound renovation. The telephone at this house was also intercepted. On a cold day in late February, whilst hiding in bracken on a hillside opposite the property, I made a video recording through the right-hand downstairs window. The client's wife was sitting at the top of the large dining table. Sitting round the table were six or seven men, apparently discussing business.

I made my way toward a number of cars parked in front of the house and continued filming.

At approximately 9.30pm the client's wife excused herself and went to another room, where she made a telephone call. This too was replayed to the client the following day. The call was to the same male as on the previous tape, and the dialogue was again very explicit.

A few days later I returned to London to prepare a listening device suitable for recording conversations in a hotel suite. I also made an aluminium bracket to clip onto the inside top of a hotel room door to enable a pinhole video camera to film the movements of people in the corridor and those entering other rooms. This equipment was to be put use in Los Angeles, where the client and his wife would be staying in a few days.

Whilst the Oscar celebrations were taking place in The Dorothy Chandler Pavilion, the equipment was set up in a nearby hotel suite. The client's wife was filmed going in to an adjoining suite. Not long after, the 'Governor' was seen to walk down the corridor and enter the client's wife's suite. The audiotapes picked up the conversation and sounds, which was not surprising as they commenced a sex session practically on top of the small microphone.

This was followed by another session in the shower. There was a lot of conversation between the couple that left in no doubt as to whom the male was.

All the tapes were given to the client's legal advisors, who prepared papers to be served by my colleague on the client's wife.

This is the story he told to me:

'I rang the doorbell to her suite. I had met her in London and in Paris. I was thinking of an occasion when I was in a limo with both of them as they were being driven to Covent Garden Opera House in London. They both sat opposite me. She was dressed in an exclusive ball gown, with a diamond-studded tiara on her head, she looked a million - no, ten million dollars. I found it so hard to believe that this was the same woman as that on the tapes.

The door to the suite opened and she was somewhat surprised when she saw me.

"Oh, hi, what brings you here? Come in sit down."

I walked into the suite and sat down on a chair and looked at her; she knew there was something up.

"What's wrong?" she asked.

I handed her an envelope, explaining it was from her husband's Legal Representative. She opened it and started read it.

"This is rubbish." She read some more and then looked up at me.

"This is not true, someone has made up this whole thing."

I explained to her that all the events had been recorded, including those in the hotel room when she was with the Governor. She then preceded to tell me that it was illegal to use 'bugs' in this particular state. I then handed her another envelope in which were the instructions of where she had to go to settle the divorce. I believe this was to be Mexico.

She then became very angry, picked up the telephone and asked for the State Trooper in the hallway to come immediately to her room. I said my farewells and left the room and waited in the corridor. The State Trooper walked down the corridor towards me. I stopped him and introduced myself as an ex-Detective from Scotland Yard. We shook hands and I explained that if he entered the suite he would find himself in the middle one of the biggest divorce battles the US had ever known. He, like most Police officers throughout the world, was wary to get involved in a matrimonial case, and with that he shook my hand, thanked me and walked off.

As he walked off down the corridor, he slowly waved his hand above his head.'

A few weeks later the equipment was returned to me and I continued with more mundane, and much less stressful work.

The divorce was finalised and from what I have read since, the lady did not go 'without'! The now ex-Governor continues to this day to deny that anything happened between him and the 'lady'.

THIRTY
WHY ME?

Sometimes, I didn't have to go looking for incidents; they came to me.

One of our bridesmaids was about to get engaged, so I offered to introduce her and her boyfriend to Tidy and Blanchard, a jewellers who advertised in the Police diary and gave discounts to police. We met up outside the shop in Hatton Garden and went to the upper floor.

Something was not quite right; the electronically-controlled mahogany doors were closed, and through the glass panels I could see two of the staff frozen in position and looking terrified. Suddenly the doors burst open and two men ran towards us, stuffing trays of diamond rings into canvas bags. We had walked into an armed robbery.

The first man pushed past me and ran down the corridor. The second tried to, but I punched him hard in his throat and he fell to the ground. I got his arm up his back in a half-Nelson. Although winded, he was still fighting .

'Kick him, kick him!' I said to the boyfriend, but he was petrified and froze, while the staff started to pile on top of me and the thief. This writhing and screaming pyramid held him down until a young PC arrived and tried to take charge.

'Nick him, nick him,' I shouted at the policeman.

'Stand up, Sir, stand up, let him go,' the policeman said to me.

As I eased my grip ever-so-slightly, the robber was off the

starting blocks. I caught hold of him by his leg and got him down again. The constable radioed for help, 'Urgent assistance required... Blanchard and Tidy, in the Garden.'

From round the corner of the corridor I could hear the sound of running feet. It sounded like a stampede. What appeared to be dozens of police officers came running down the narrow corridor. It was all caps, helmets and truncheons. They were bouncing off the walls, falling over each other in their eagerness to get to the robbery. It looked like a scene from some old Keystone Cops film.

'Where's the robbery?' said one.

'It's over,' I said. 'This is one of them!'

The scrawny Moroccan robber was pushed against the wall and held by two PCs. He began to explain in broken English that he had been chasing the 'bad man' who was robbing the shop.

'He was one of them. You lying fuckpig. Not so fucking brave now, you slimy foreign Maltese poncing bastard,' shouted one of the sales staff, a good old-fashioned East End girl.

An older PC who had seen it all before put his face right up close to the robber.

'Shut your fucking face. You're nicked. Put this arsehole in the van.'

Four officers bundled the robber down the corridor.

The East End girl, for all her bravado, was shaken and crying. The officer put his arm round her shoulder.

'Madam, you were wrong. Number one, I don't think he's Maltese, most likely Moroccan. Secondly, I doubt if he's a ponce, more likely a robber.'

He gave her a gentle pat on her shoulder, smiling as he let her go.

A few days later I went to Holborn Police Station, where I learnt that the Moroccan, along with one other, had been arrested and charged with robbery. My offer to provide a statement was never taken up.

My reward? It's still in the pipeline, although I did receive a pair of earrings for my wife, compliments of the jewellers.

Incidents continued. I was in Wales doing an insurance investigation. It was the usual thing, someone trying to rip-off an

'Yes, guv, what can I do you for?'

'I'm trying to trace an old woman by the name of Old, Betty Old, she was supposed to have worked here.'

The assistant looked over his shoulder.

'Dad there's a geezer 'ere looking for old Betty.'

A middle-aged man came out of the back shop with a mug of tea cupped in his hands.

'Yes guv?'

I explained the story to him.

'If it's the same old bird, she did work but left about ten years ago.'

'Have you any idea where she lives?'

'No, but the guv'nor of the pub across the road, he should know - she works there as a cleaner.'

I walked over the road and walked into the bar. Apart from a few pensioners playing cards in the corner, the place was empty. A man stood behind the bar engrossed in the *Sun* crossword. He looked up, dropping his well-chewed betting-shop pen.

'Yes, guv, what can I do you for?'

I thought to myself, is this the best line of 'patter' they can produce in this area?

I ordered a drink. It was poured and grudgingly pushed in front of me. I paid, and the man put the money in the open drawer of the cash register. He buried his head in the crossword, lit up a cigarette, took along draw on it, and then placed it in the ashtray and looked at me.

'Beat on one four-letter word.'

'What's that?'

'Four across, 'Conclusion in music'. Sod it.' He folded his paper and put it under the bar.

'Try, 'Coda'.'

He reached for his paper, opened out and filled in the space.

'You're right, it was Coda, you a musician?'

'No, I'm a private investigator.'

'What, like the Old Bill?'

'Yes, something like that, is the boss about?'

'That's me'

I relayed the story of 'Betty'.

'Oh, you're just too late, she left us last Friday.'

'What, dead?'

'Nah, we had a party for her, she retired.'

He gave me her address; I thanked him and started to walk out of the pub.

'Oh, mate, how did you know that coda thing?'

'It's a long story, all to do with a Sally-Ann Band. Bye.'

He looked at me with a totally puzzled look on his face.

I walked down the road to a block of council flats and knocked on number 37. The door opened and there was my client's 'wife', only forty years older. I couldn't believe my eyes, six hours after taking instructions I was looking at my client's mother. I did not have to ask question, they were like peas in a pod.

'You're Betty Old?'

'Yes, who are you?'

'Jim Smith, did you have a daughter forty years ago?'

'Come in.'

We sat and had a cup of tea and I switched on my tape recorder. I explained and described how her daughter looked and how many children she had. I tried to be as diplomatic and sympathetic as possible.

'You know, I often wondered what happened to that little bleeder.'

She then went on to describe another two children she had 'given away'. She could only guess as to who the fathers could be.

I have never reunited families without having a long chat with the clients and the 'lost one' beforehand. This was particularly difficult, due to the two extreme lifestyles of both parties. The daughter had been brought up by kind adoptive parents and had married a successful businessman. They had lovely and well-educated children.

Two or three days later, I reunited mother and daughter at the flat in Staines. The daughter was wearing a mink coat and looking a million dollars. I knocked on the door, which was opened by Betty. Both stood looking at each other. There was silence, then uniformed female officers, who looked as if they had been thrown out of the Russian shot put team for being too ugly. They examined my passport and walked over to me, the larger of the two carrying my passport.

She stopped in front of me, looked at my passport and nodded.

'Come with us, Mr James Smith.'

One walked off as we followed behind her. I remember thinking to myself, 'With an arse that size there must be a trunk at the other end.'

She clutched the side of her tunic and pulled it up, revealing a large bunch of keys clipped onto the side of her skirt. She pulled them off, searched the bunch for a key and opened a door of an office.

'In here please, Mr James Smith.'

I walked into the room and looked around. It was dirty and in need of decorating. There was a metal table and two old wooden chairs. I was shown to one of them.

'Sit down, Mr James Smith.'

'Elephant arse' sat opposite me. Nobody spoke as she thumbed through my passport. She looked up.

'I see you are a photographer.'

I had completely forgotten that I had shown my occupation as 'photographer' on my passport.

'Yes, photographer.'

'Why are you coming to Malta at this time?'

'For a holiday.'

'A holiday, at this time?'

'Is the weather not too good?'

'Yes, the weather is fine. What type of pictures do you take?'

'Weddings, calendars, buildings, you know that type of thing.'

'Whom do you work for?'

'Anyone who wants pictures taken; if they have the money, I do the work.'

'What companies do you work for?'

'I work for myself.'

'So, if a newspaper says "Mr James, here is some money go to

Malta and take some pictures of the troubles", you would go?'

'No, I don't do that type of pictures, it's too dangerous for me. I prefer looking at nice lady models in the studio. Understand?'

The questions went on for about another ten minutes and eventually ended with the warning, 'We will be watching you. We had to send your BBC man home, don't do anything to spoil your holiday. Goodbye.'

I collected my case which had been opened and searched. They had paid no apparent attention to the pictures I had copied of Michael and Joseph.

I called a taxi and was taken to my hotel. The only star rating this place had was 'disastar'.

I was checked in by an unshaven receptionist dressed in a dirty vest, jeans and a pair of sandals.

I went to my room. It was clean but sparse. I had to clean my teeth with lager and toothpaste, as there was only a brown sludge coming out of the ill-fitting water tap. I crashed out on the top of the bed with my camera equipment under the pillow. This wasn't like the American private investigators I had seen in films; they always had a gun under their pillow, not a Pentax camera.

The following morning I arrived at reception to complain about my room.

'Ah! Jimmy Smith, Don Murphy's friend. He told me you were coming. I am sorry the idiots last night put you in the wrong room. I have a suite for you, same price.' It was the hotel proprietor.

Don Murphy was a hotel owner in Bracknell in Berkshire who frequently visited Malta and, knowing that I was working on a very tight budget, had suggested this hotel.

I was taken to the 'suite'. It was a bigger room with hot and cold running water and a balcony overlooking the town. I suppose that made it a suite in this hotel.

Michael and Joseph's surname was 'Debono'. I started searching the telephone book; everyone in Malta seemed to be called Debono. I decided to walk round the town for any clues as to their possible whereabouts. As I walked round the narrow streets, I came across the local police station. I spoke to the officer who was working behind the counter.

to my lips and indicated to be quiet. He stopped and stared at me. Other members of staff were now looking to see what was going on. Michael was totally unaware that I was behind him.

He suddenly turned round as he pulled the wooden pole from the oven.

'Michael, Michael Debono?'

'Yes, what?'

'Do you know this boy?'

I held up the photo of him as a boy.

'That's me.'

He then looked up and saw Joseph.

'What's, what's going on?'

'I've come from your mother,' I said.

'Mum?'

Joseph walked over. We all hugged as the bakers stood looking at the spectacle of three grown men hugging each other. Eventually the boss came over to find out what was going on. As soon as he was told he started to take off Michael's work jacket. We all knew there was no more bread going to be baked by Michael that night. The boss walked back to the other workers and spoke to them. We left the bakery and walked up the street, me in the middle being held tightly by two lost sons. A round of applause and cheers echoed out of the bakery.

We sat talking into the early hours, and gradually their past came out. When staying in Govan, their mother had gone into hospital. Their father took them to Wales with the 'woman upstairs'. Many stories were told to them as what had happened to their mother. Some time later, while their father was at work, his girlfriend collapsed and died as she stood working at the kitchen sink. Their father took them to Malta to live.

After a few years, he too died and the boys were left on their own, thousands of miles from their mother and not knowing the truth. They were brought up by a relative in Malta who was subsequently jailed for killing her husband. The boys were yet again left on their own, to be brought up by other relatives.

I returned to my hotel room and stood on the balcony overlooking the night sky.

'Thanks, God,' I thought.

The following morning the boys arrived at the hotel and we went up to my 'suite'.

Joseph got up and opened the sliding door onto the veranda.

'Jim, you are not going to believe this. I used to work in this hotel and I used to stand on this very balcony and pray that some day my mother would come to me.'

A prayer answered. Michael took a picture of us on the spot.

That evening I telephoned Betty.

'Hello, Betty, it's Jim Smith.'

'Oh, hi, Jim, have you found them?'

'Hold on a wee minute, I've got someone here who wants to speak to you.'

I handed the phone to Joseph.

'Hello, Mum, it's Joseph, I'm with Michael.'

Everything else was lost in tears.

The family were reunited in Malta.

Over the years I lost contact with them. However, when writing this book I had to find the family again. I sent a letter to a 'M. Debono' in England and two days later, and twenty-three years to the date that had I found them, Michael telephoned me. It was with sadness that I heard that Joseph had died of a heart attack some years earlier. Betty, too, had died.

Michael is living with his wife and his grown up family in England.

We will keep in touch.

THIRTY-THREE
'BIRCHIE'

MAGPIES

One for sorrow, Two for joy,
Three for a girl, Four for a boy
Five for silver, Six for GOLD,
Seven for a SECRET,
as yet untold.

The Flying Squad at New Scotland Yard, situated on the fourth floor in the Victoria block in Victoria Street in London, has always been steeped in mystery to the general public. There were more characters in the Squad than the rest of the Met. They worked and played hard. Villains feared 'The Sweeney'.

Nicky Birch, a former Squad officer and the son of a vicar, was one such character who, after his retirement, took up employment as the security director of a major distribution company. He was a terrier when it came to catching thieves.

Nick was a red haired-fireball, who was the master of under-expression. Nick could never drive past a magpie without raising his hand in a salute and reciting his favourite 'Magpie Rhyme'. It was just one of Nick's idiosyncrasies.

I once saw Nick at the scene of an attempted armed robbery. One of the robbers, who had been knocked to the ground and disarmed by him, lay spread-eagled on the ground. Nick, astride his chest, was holding him by the throat. The robber's eyes were bulging, whilst Nick, with his free hand, index finger outstretched in front of his face, was whispering, 'You naughty boy, you must stop this silly nonsense. You're nicked!'

This, to a 'geezer' who a few seconds earlier would have blown Nick's head off with the sawn-off shotgun lying at his side. Villains to Nick were 'little monkeys.' Every successful operation was 'Tickety Boo'.

I got to know him well after he left the police.

One day my office phone rang, and before I could give my number, Nick had already started.

'Birch here, are you free for a knife and fork job?'

Nick wanted to meet me for lunch and give me instructions for a new assignment.

'Yes, what time?'

'One o'clock at The Rossetti?

'Yes, OK.'

'Tickety Boo.'

The dialling tone informed me Nick had finished the conversation. I looked down the mouthpiece, sat for a few seconds and then placed the handset on the cradle. That was just his way... hyperactive when there were thieves to be caught.

The Rossetti, a restaurant in the St John's Wood area of London, was bustling with business people having lunch when I arrived. Nick was at the bar.

'Ah, Mr Smith, what are you having?

'A Spritzer.'

'Tony, Spritzer for Mr Smith, thank you.'

'I've got a table booked. We will be joined by a couple of good chaps from the RCS.' (Regional Crime Squad)

We sat down at our table and were soon joined by the two officers. Nick introduced me to them, and it did not take him long to get into the 'story'.

'In our South London Depot, some little scallywags are having our booze away. I've been down there at various times but can't see anything untoward. I can't get too close as they all know me. How do you fancy working in there as a picker?' 'What's a picker?

'A picker works in our distribution branches; they are given orders to load onto pallets. The goods can be anything from bog

A quick stop down the road to meet with another mate, the number plates were then changed, and off it goes to the 'run in'. 'Ah! Bisto!' Another load of goods stolen from the depot.

Nick kept a close watch on the documentation. Ten days later he had traced another 'moody' list and contacted me, his voice full of excitement.

'I'll be down there tomorrow morning with the cavalry (a Crime Squad team). Keep your head down, see you soon.'

He was having another adrenalin rush.

Next morning, *New York, New York* was interrupted.

'Staff announcement, Staff announcement. All pickers go to the staff canteen for a briefing now please... Thank you.'

Amidst the moans and obscenities we walked towards the staircase leading to the canteen. Standing at the bottom of the stairs were two people from the personnel department.

'The following people come with me.'

Myself, together with another three were led off to the canteen. We were addressed by a member of the personnel department.

'Gentlemen, this will not take long, Mr Birch, our Security Director, will address you in a few minutes.'

And with that he sat down.

I looked out of the window. A Police van was being loaded with my four work 'colleagues', all handcuffed and looking forlorn, giving the obligatory shrug of one shoulder as they were ushered in. It drove out of the yard followed by two Crime Squad cars. Sat in the rear of one was Nicky, with a broad smile on his face.

'Gentlemen, unfortunately Mr Birch has been called away. We will have to postpone the meeting to a future time. Sorry, back to work. Thank you.'

'What was all that about? They couldn't organize a piss up in a brewery, this lot!'

Nick didn't need a brewery!

That night we met at The Rossetti. Nick was at the bar with some of the Crime Squad who had arrested my 'chums'.

'Spritzer for the Glaswegian hooligan, and gentlemen, please do not call him a 'Scots arsehole' or you may discover the power of flour power!'

With that I was introduced to the full team.

'We nicked the driver, Shagnasty. He was wanted on warrant. Your four mates are well-captured, two of them have put their hands up, the boys got the 'slaughter' (where stolen goods are split). With more 'hooky gear' stashed there, a nice little tickle and they haven't sussed you. It's time for you to be 'arrested' and returned to Glasgow. That'll be next Tuesday, so don't turn up. I'll spin them a yarn.'

'Another Spritzer?'

'Why not?'

'Tony, a Spritzer for the Scottish gentleman!'

Over the next few years I had the pleasure to work with Nick, during which time we were responsible for the arrest of many criminals and the recovery of hundreds of thousands of pounds-worth of stolen property. These arrests included a gang who were responsible for the theft of the largest amount of computer chips stolen in Scotland. I enjoyed my time working in and around Glasgow; there wasn't a day passed without us being creased up with laughter. Glasgow has always been a city full of comedians. Glaswegians will converse with complete strangers and pass the time of day with a good laugh, it's known as 'the patter'.

What is the patter?

On a wet, cold winter's morning myself and two colleagues hailed a taxi, which duly pulled across the traffic and stopped at the kerbside, the windscreen wipers showering us with what appeared to be gallons of water in their attempt to clear the horizontal rain.

'Jump in, boys.'

Boys? There was none of us under fifty.

We gave the driver our destination and set off. He continued talking through the gap in the glass partition.

'Up on business, are we?'

'Yes.'

'Well, I hope you're no in a hurry, the traffic is murder and it's no helped by these Polis, they do that every mornin'.

'What's that?'

'Them there.'

He pointed ahead at two police officers sitting astride two of the biggest horses you've ever seen. Strathclyde Police use Clydesdales in their mounted division. The Clydesdale is one of the largest breeds of horses in the world, its hooves look like hairy dustbin lids.

'Every mornin' they come up, supposed to helpin' the traffic. They cause more problems than all the cars put together. That Polis on outside horse is Big Tam, he's been on that horse for years.'

The taxi crept slowly forward, its speed determined by the slow pace of the horses.

We continued talking amongst ourselves.

'Oh, did you see that boys?'

'No sorry, what was that?'

'Shit, the horse has just dumped the biggest heap of shit I've ever seen, see if ma wee dug has a wee shite in the street the Polis are after me.'

Sure enough, there was a dump of considerable proportions which our driver took delight in driving over. Big Tam, towering above the traffic waved the traffic on. Our cab pulled alongside him as the traffic lights changed to red. We stopped, our driver lowered his window and put his head out.

'Mornin', Tam.'

'Oh, its yerself, Wullie, how's it goin'?'

'Okay, except for ma suspension.'

'What's the problem?'

'I think it's knackered bumping over that heap of shite your horse dropped in the middle of the street.'

'Wullie, go back and get it and put it on your rhubarb.'

'We have custard with ours, Tam.'

'Wullie, if this horse could shite custard, it would be working in the Central Hotel. All the best Wullie.'

With that the two mounted officers turned right and cantered off, allowing the traffic to flow freely.

That's 'the patter' - a good laugh, nobody harmed, work carried out and the day passes quickly.

Another phone call.

'Birch here, I've got a nice one for you. Rossetti? Two o'clock, OK?'

'OK.'

Little did I know then that this particular 'nice one' would lead to a major breakthrough in organised crime within this country, Spain and the USA, and open up the first serious investigation into what became known as the Costa Del Crime.

THIRTY-FOUR
A HOUSE IN WORONZOW ROAD

I met up with Nick in The Rossetti. As usual, no time was wasted in niceties.

'This job is a bit different, the guy I'll introduce you to has got in with a right tasty bunch. I'll let him tell you all about it when he comes in. To be quite honest, I do not know the full SP myself. Ah! here he comes now.'

I saw a man - in his 50s, medium build, dapper-looking - stride across the carpet towards us. He had an air about him that picqued one's curiosity, and I noticed that some of the other patrons took notice of his arrival.

'Hi, Nick.' he said.

Before I could say anything, he reached out and firmly shook my hand.

'You must be Jim. I'm Winston Skelley. Nick's told me a lot about you. Let's take a seat.'

We sat at a corner and ate some lunch. Winston, dressed in a smart suit and wearing RAF cufflinks, spoke with a soft, cultured English accent. On close inspection - but not too close - it was obvious that he was sporting a toupee. As the conversation proceeded, it was clear that he had known Nick for some years. Winston had once managed a hotel in the Bayswater Road area of London which was a watering hole for both villains and the Flying Squad.

Winston soon got to the point.

'I have a little business venture running at the moment - it's to do with investing capital from a gold project that I'm looking after. Unfortunately, some rather heavy criminal elements have taken an interest in it and are trying to make contact with me. I have made it quite clear to them that I want nothing to do with them, and that Her Majesty's Customs Officers are at my house and are also secretly photographing all visitors. What I would like you to do is attend my house and answer the telephone as if you are a Customs Officer.'

'Tell me, Winston, what do Customs Officers sound like?' I asked.

'Like you. Nick tells me you have a surveillance van. I would like you to park it just down the road from my property and that will complete my story.'

'I'll need to know a bit more before I can commit myself,' I replied.

'That's okay. Come back to the house and I will fill in the details.'

Winston settled the bill, and outside Nick gave me a knowing wink and drove off.

We arrived back at the house in Woronzow Road, situated in an exclusive part of St John's Wood in North London where all the properties are worth at least two million pounds. Winston's place was a large white semi-detached three-storey property surrounded by a walled garden.

We were greeted by his French wife, Joelle, who led us in through the large double-doors, served coffee and left us in the large lounge with its floor-to-ceiling French windows at the far end. We sat down in plush chairs.

The phone rang several times. On each occasion, Winston pointed to it and nodded.

I picked up the receiver.

'Mr Skelley's house,' I said.

'Is he there?' a voice asked.

'Who?'

'Winston.'

THIRTY-FIVE

THE NOLANS

Was Winston a villain? He certainly was involved with shady characters, but seemed detached from them in some way. Why did he want me involved? Surely, not just to answer the phone and park a van outside his house.

Two days later I arrived back at his house, and as we sat down in the lounge Joelle appeared with the coffee.

'Good morning, Jimee,' she said. Her French accent made 'Jimmy' sound a bit special, unlike the "see you Jimmy" of Glasgow.

'Well, have you thought any more about taking on the case?' Winston asked, as he stared straight at me.

'Yes, but I can't help thinking that there is a lot more to this,' I replied.

'You're dead right. I have dug out more papers to enable me to fill you in. You see, initially, I was approached to invest funds that they had because of my experience in selling gold on the market. Robertson had started out with a few thousand pounds, but within weeks he had changed this into hundreds-of-thousands of pounds he wanted to invest.'

I was now tempted to walk out on the spot. Winston was a hard read. But curiosity was getting the better of me. On one hand, I was thinking 'curiosity killed the cat', while on the other I was hearing 'satisfaction brought it back'! His story was intriguing. The people he was talking about were some of the 'prominent' ones I had sat in the rear of an observation vehicle covertly photographing just a few years before. They didn't know me, but I had come to know them as they went about their criminal activities.

Winston lit up another cigarette and continued.

'I took Robertson to Rome to meet a Monsignor Mario Formisari, a senior person in the Vatican. The purpose of the visit was to introduce Robertson to charity dioceses of the church that would be prepared to sell him gold internationally in the sort of quantities he was after. The funds would be from his own monies and that of his associates. There was a total of somewhere in the region £2 million. The money would be rolled over and realize a profit. Now we come to the bit that immediately raised my suspicions. They did not want to pay any form of duty bringing it into the UK, i.e. to avoid paying VAT. I explained to them that if they became registered as bullion dealers they would only pay VAT when they sold the gold on. This seemed to satisfy them. I also introduced them to a Mr Sania Cateeb, the head dealer of the Arab Bank Ltd in St Martins-le-Grand in the City. It was decided on his advice to buy Krugerrands, as there was no VAT on them. He also set up an overseas corporation for the purchase of gold. The people involved in this were a man named James Marsden, Robertson and this Jimmy Jeffries, a Scotsman, and Marsden's driver, a man called Dennis - although I don't believe he played an active part. Various transactions took place with money going through my solicitors. One day, Cateeb asked me if I realized that these people could be melting down the gold and selling it on and charging VAT, which they kept. I thought about it, and it all fitted.'

We sat for ages going through documents, and it soon became clear that this team had set up numerous limited companies. Gold ingots were being made from the smelted imported gold coins, which were then sold to bullion dealers in the City. The various companies did this over a three-month period, after which they 'upped-sticks' and vanished prior to paying the VAT owed to the Government. They had about seventy companies running at any given time. Each company was making 15½% 'profit', totalling hundreds of thousands of pounds each week.

'Now, Jimmy, what I want you to do is get pictures of these people to enable me to identify who they are before I go to the money. In his financial dealings, the man seemed to have balls of brass.

So why didn't I just pull out? After all, I was only working on a daily rate. I suppose the answer is that I was enjoying the thrill of the chase.

And as it transpired, Winston and Joelle would assist me in my next case involving a family in desperation.

THIRTY-SEVEN
MORE PRECIOUS THAN GOLD

Whilst waiting for further developments from Winston I was at the office catching up with the rest of my work. Compared to the gold saga, my usual pursuits were sorely lacking the excitement factor. For example, insurance fraud surveillance that kept me away from home, my wife and two sons. Or the nuts, like the woman who suspected her husband of having an affair. When I met her she seemed normal, then the calls to me started. 'The bird has flown the nest' was her code to tell me her husband had left the house. The poor man was only ever going to a local social club to get out of the house. Who could blame him?

Or there were real nuts, people who seemed to make genuine enquiries that they were unwilling to discuss on the telephone. When I met such 'clients', they insisted that they were being kept under observation by 'people from outer space' or 'MI6'. The peculiar enquiries usually stemmed from my listing in the *Yellow Pages*. However, all shared one factor in common, whether as private individuals or as a representative of a company - the willingness to pour out their deepest secrets to me; secrets they wouldn't tell their best friend, spouse or priest.

It was a Tuesday afternoon, at about 2.30, when the phone rang. I reached over and turned down the brass band music I had playing in the background.

'Is that the detective agency?' a male voice enquired.

'Yes,' I answered.

'Do you bring children back from abroad?' he asked.

'Depends on what you mean by 'back'.'

'They are being held in Spain.'

'What do you mean, being held?'

'I want them snatched and brought back to Britain.'

'I don't do that type of work,' I said.

'What if they are in moral danger?' he asked.

Whether it was the Geordie accent, or the intonation of his voice, or something else - perhaps a hint of fear mixed with sincerity - my intuition was to hear more about the problem.

But before I could answer, he blurted out: 'They are my grandkids, and the scumbag of a father is holding them hostage in Spain. I need your help. Please come and speak to me. I'll pay you.'

'I'll come and see you,' I said. 'Give me your address, I don't charge for consultations.'

Two hours later, I arrived at a 1950s mid-terraced house on the outskirts of Reading. I was shown in and introduced to the man who had phoned me, Bob Johnson; tall, thin, aged about sixty-five, with a face of one who had lived a full life. All about him were tables and shelves covered with mementoes and family photographs, as well as around a dozen members of his extended family - children, grandchildren, brothers, sisters, nephews and nieces - even a couple of toddlers. There was a 'waiting for the hearse to arrive' atmosphere in the crowded room, and all their attention was now directed towards me - the man from the Yellow Pages.

I was then introduced to an attractive 35-year-old woman sitting in the corner of the room. I saw that her face had been battered.

'This is Linda, my daughter,' Bob said. 'The scumbag did that to her and he's got the kids: Amanda, who's thirteen, Maxine, eight, and Emma, three. He did that to her, my daughter. I knew he was a scumbag when I met him. And to think I used to help these Spanish bastards during the Civil War.'

The room then exploded with a cacophony of voices.

'Poor Emma, the wee bairn… three years of age and with that shit.'

'Don't forget Amanda and Maxine, they're only babies…'

'I'm not, it's all so confusing…'

I heard a woman's voice from the back of the room. I hadn't noticed her before, she was middle-aged and slumped in a chair with her tear-stained face in her hands.

'Oh, God, please, please keep them in your precious hands and bring them home safely to the fold of the family,' she said. A sincere prayer between herself and God.

'…that evil dago is doing things to the girls he shouldn't.'

'…bastard!'

I had witnessed lots of 'domestics' before, and normally I would have tried to establish some calm and order. But here, the pent-up emotion needed to be let out. I was going to be expected to have the answers - I didn't even have the questions.

Eventually, a voice called out through the crowd, 'Do you want a drink?'

'A cup of tea will do fine, no milk,' I said. 'Let's sit down and tell me the story. Now take it easy.'

'Dad, you tell him. I can't go through it all again.' said Linda.

As she turned round, I could see swelling to her face, a bloodshot eye and areas where the skin was slightly broken. The bruising looked like it was still coming out. Linda was pretty, but not a pretty sight.

'Who did that?' I asked.

Linda didn't answer. She just dropped her head and wept.

'The scumbag who's got the wains. Her so-called husband, and the father of her children,' Bob said.

'OK, Bob, let's start at the beginning,' I suggested.

'OK, but before I start, read this.'

He handed me a small piece of folded toilet paper. On the outside it read 'Goodbye Mum'. A little cushion had been drawn with the words, 'I love you'. Inside it read, 'P.S. Please hurry and try to get us back home, I will love you always and give my love to the family.' It ended by saying 'I will kill Dad.' Below there were ten kisses drawn. The writing was Amanda's.

'Have you thought of anything?' he asked.

'OK, this is a plan, I think it will work. I know a man by the name of Winston. He is living in Lourdes with his wife and family. I suggest that Linda and I fly to Lourdes... Linda, are the children on your passport?'

'Yes, it's a new passport,' she said.

'OK, we fly to Lourdes and stay overnight. I will arrange for a private aircraft to fly us down to Cuatro Vientos, it's a small private airfield just outside Madrid. I'll have a friend from London - Nick the Greek - (laughter passed round the family) - waiting for us on our arrival at the airfield. He'll have hired an estate car and have gotten an extra set of keys cut. We'll all drive to a nearby café or restaurant. Nick will then go in alone, have a drink, and make himself known. Linda and I will then be driving the seventy miles southwest to Pulgar in the hire car using the spare keys. In the meantime Nick, having sat there for a couple of hours, will leave his set of keys on the bar and make an exit. He'll then come back approximately thirty minutes later.'

'Why?' asked Bob.

'If anything should go wrong with us, it will mean that he'll have an alibi that gives him a chance to get off the hook.'

Eyebrows were raised, heads nodded, and I continued.

'Linda, is there any special spot where the children go to away from the house?'

'Well, we walked to a bridge and fed the donkeys in the field. The kids loved it.'

'OK, this Friday when the scumbag phones (even I had now got into the vernacular), will you get a chance to speak to Amanda on her own?'

'Maybe, last time he let me speak to all of the children,' Linda said.

'OK, this is what you will say to Amanda: next Friday at 3.00pm, go to the place where you fed the donkeys. Tell her to stay close together with her sisters, but she mustn't tell Emma or Maxine what we are doing. Tell her that at three o'clock, a man with a red sweater and a blue denim hat will walk past them and he will say, "I'm Jim". She must then take her sisters by the hand and follow him. Tell her not to speak to him, that he will tell her what to do, and that he will have a car, OK?'

'OK, but write it down for me.'

'Don't worry, Linda, it will all be done for you – this is just the beginning. We will then drive off, back to the plane, then fly to Lourdes and safety. By the time the scumbag looks for the children, hopefully we will already be back in Lourdes. Now there is one problem here – cash. We have air fares, private plane, the pilot, hotels, car hire and Nick the Greek,' I said.

Bob kicked in.

'Bonny lad, the family have all chipped in money and it's not a problem. There is one problem though: Linda is terrified of flying. She has never done it, that's why they sailed to Spain.'

The next couple of days were spent preparing instructions for Nick, a script for Linda and Bob, and confirmation with Winston that everything was OK with accommodation and the pilot etc. I had a couple of meetings with Nick at the St George's Bar in the Hilton in Park Lane, London. He and I went over and over the plan until we were satisfied. I also had a further meeting with Linda before she had to give Amanda the instructions.

Friday, 6th May, at Reading… back in Bob's house. 4.30pm… Some of Bob's family have returned, and we all sit waiting for the phone call. I have given Linda her script and she has read it over and over; now her hands were shaking.

'Will you answer the phone, Dad?' she asked.

'Yes, but it will take all I've got not to blow…'

The phone rang.

'Bob Johnson, no, she's out at the moment. I'll tell her when she gets in. Yes, she'll ring you, OK, bye.'

'Who was that?' Linda asked.

'Sandra or somebody.'

'What did she want?'

'Wanted to know if your house is up for sale.'

The phone rang again.

'Bob Johnson.'

Anger flooded over his face.

'Hold on, I'll get her. Linda, it's for you.'

Bob shouted as if she was in the next room. His face was white with temper, emotion and frustration. He waited a few moments and then handed the phone to Linda.

'Hello… How do you expect me to be?' Linda asked. 'Be reasonable! You think you're being reasonable?'

I held my finger to my mouth, indicating with my other hand to keep calm.

'Yes, I've been to the estate agents… Yes, it's on the market.'

I pointed to her script.

'How are the children?'

'Yes, for a quick sale… It doesn't happen overnight. What do you mean, "They're OK"?'

Bob stuffed his half-smoked cigarette out in the ashtray. He too was pointing at the script.

'Yes, yes, put them on. Emma darling, how are you, OK? Good girl. Mummy's doing work for Daddy. I love you. Maxine, how are you darling? Good, I've got to do work for Daddy and then we will all be together. I know darling, and I'm missing you too. I love you. Amanda, listen carefully. Is your Dad near you? Just say 'yes' or 'no'. Good. What I am going to say you must not tell Maxine or Emma. I will be coming to get you home… no, no don't speak just listen… please! What do you do during the day? You don't see your dad or his family until when? Six o'clock? OK, now listen darling…'

The atmosphere in the room was electric. Most people were sitting with their faces buried in their hands, others stood staring out of the window. All were scared to breath or move.

'Next Friday at ten minutes to three in the afternoon, go to the bridge where you fed the donkeys. OK? A man in a red sweater will walk past, he will say, "I'm Jim." Don't speak to him, just follow him, and then just do what he tells you to do. You mustn't tell Maxine or Emma because they may tell your dad. Do you understand? Good girl. Now tell me again what I said. Yes, good. No, no. Ten minutes to three. Okay! Okay! Don't speak, love you.'

The phone had evidently been taken from Amanda.

'Oh, she was just asking about her grandfather. Yes, I'll get the bloody house sold. Next Friday when you phone can you make it a bit later, I have an appointment with the solicitor… the bloody house, what do you think?'

Everyone in the room was hoping Linda would keep her temper.

'OK. Seven pm. Yes! Yes, bye.'

She hung up phone.

'Oh God, I forgot to say you would be wearing a denim hat.'

Linda walked out of the room and we could hear her crying behind a closed door.

This was to be the last contact with the children before Friday, May 13th. We were asking so much of a thirteen-year-old.

Bob looked at me. The anger on his face could not be hidden. He lit another cigarette; his hands were shaking.

'OK, Bob,' I said, 'we have to go with the plan. It's a risk, and having six men on the job would be better. Let me explain the problems before Linda comes back. Number one problem is her fear of flying, although I am sure she will get over this. Number two is the everyday problems - the car breaks down, accident, puncture etc. But honestly, Bob, in my heart of hearts I feel we can pull this off. If you go through solicitors and the Hague Convention, there is no saying what will happen to these children. This father is one very bad man.'

Bob looked up, drew on his cigarette, inhaled the smoke, and with a firm, yet sad, voice said, 'Go for it.'

He blew the smoke out, pulled himself out of his armchair and reached into the cupboard next to him, taking out a brown envelope.

'Jim, there is seven thousand pounds in there, let's get started,' he said.

'I'll give you a receipt,' I said.

'I don't want a receipt. I'm trusting you with my grandchildren and you're bringing them back to me.'

Many things had to be done before leaving the UK, but eventually, on Wednesday, 11th May, 1983, I was up early, saying goodbye to my family and finally setting off to collect Linda.

As I drove into the crescent I could see her standing at the front door with her Dad. I had made up my mind - straight in and out - no time for emotion or change of mind. She looked a nervous wreck. I am sure that she too was aware that if anything went wrong at Pulgar, like the scumbag or his family sussing us, we would be in the lion's den. As I walked up the path, Linda was kissing her dad goodbye.

'Passports, clothing?' I asked.

'Yes, I've checked them over and over and over again, Jim,' Linda said.

'OK, let's go.

I picked up her case and made my way to the car. I didn't want to get too close to the family. I kept saying to myself throughout this: stay detached; stay detached.

As Linda got into the car Bob closed the door, put his head through the open window, and held her face in his hands.

'You'll be OK, love. Look after her, Jim,' he said.

It was a quick drive down the motorway to Heathrow. I had one last look at the car and thought: I hope I see you on Saturday.

'Oh, well, Linda, that's it until Saturday,' I said.

Linda managed a slight smile, or perhaps it was more of a grimace. We made our way to Terminal One, a strange place for her, and checked-in.

'Let's go and have a coffee while we wait for the flight to be called,' I said.

'What happens if the Greek guy doesn't turn up with the car?' Linda asked.

'Sugar?' I asked.

'I mean, we would be stuck in Madrid and the kids would be standing waiting… What happens if Amanda's forgotten the day?'

'Linda, we will be OK. The police have an expression - if the cat hadn't pissed, it would have burst. So no more what ifs, please.'

Linda went off to the toilet, and while she was away I had time to think. If this blew out, the family would lose the children and the seven grand. And there was no saying when I would see my family next, as I had no doubt that the Spanish authorities would not be too lenient on anyone involved in taking children out of their country, even for the best of reasons. I also had no doubt if it went wrong, the scumbag would allege I had kidnapped them. Being slapped-up in a Spanish gaol would be a distinct possibility. However, I vowed to remain undaunted in the attempt to get these children back to safety.

As Linda returned, the flight was called. Her legs were like jelly as we walked to the gate.

I tried to reassure her.

'Just stay next to me and you will be OK. It's the safest means of travel. You will no sooner be up than we will be touching down. Oh, what's that?' I asked.

'What?' asks Linda.

'A pilot with a guide dog,' I said.

'Where, where?' Linda asked, looking about the room.

'Over there - oh, you've just missed him, he's gone in to fly our plane.'

With that, I received a punch in the arm from her. Maybe she was relaxing a little.

We got on to the aircraft and into our seats. It looked as if Linda was trying to see what was inside the armrests, as she dug her fingers into them and was pulling them so hard. Soon the plane was taxiing and we were airborne. I had never been with a client so nervous.

Finally, the announcement came up: 'Ladies and gentlemen we will shortly be arriving at Charles de Gaulle airport.'

Linda looked at me. 'That wasn't as bad as I expected.'

'Didn't I tell you so?'

'Oh, well, I feel I can cope in a plane of this size. How big is the one into Spain?'

'Substantial,' I replied.

We were soon out of the plane and into a taxi to book in at Orly's Holiday Inn. We agreed to meet two hours later in the bar.

'Try to have a lie down and get some sleep,' I suggested.

I went to my room. Over and over in my head the plans were rolling. Eventually, I convinced myself that everything looked OK. Besides, there was little more I could do at this point. I fell into a deep sleep and was suddenly awakened with a start, sitting bolt upright. Nick the Greek was in Amsterdam, dressed in his pyjamas. 'Nick, Nick, what the hell are you doing?' I said aloud.

My heart was thumping… What made me dream that?

When I walked downstairs to the dimly-lit bar Linda was already there. We ordered drinks, and as the barman served us he gave us a knowing look accompanied by a wry smile and a little smirk, implying a dirty weekend. If only he had known.

Linda then started to talk about her father.

'You know he saw a lot of action during the war. He was on coasters, up and down from Sunderland way, bringing down coal and other things to London. His ships were attacked. He was shipwrecked and rescued on a number of occasions. I remember him telling me about his ship being hit by a German plane - the ship rolled over and his best mate was sucked into the funnel. There was a tremendous explosion, and his friend was blown back out of the funnel like a bloody human-cannonball. You know, Jim, Dad told us that the guy survived.'

Linda looked down in deep thought as she ran her fingers round the glass. She stopped and looked up towards me.

'Do you think the kids will be OK, Jim?'

'Yes, I have no doubt they will be. Come on let's eat.'

She picked at her food and pushed the half-finished meal to the middle of the table. 'Sorry, I must go and speak to Dad.'

I sat thinking things over. Could Amanda keep her secret? Did she talk in her sleep? Would she remember the day? My thoughts were disrupted as Linda returned to the table. She had been crying, and wiped her eyes and said to me:

'Dad's worried, I can tell. I told him we are OK and everything is fine.'

'OK, let's get you to your room, we'll meet, say, for 8.00am.'

At 5.00am the following morning I was wide awake. I showered and was downstairs by 6.30. By 8.30 there was no sign of Linda. I went to her room where she was sitting on the bed, fully-clothed, her packed bag by her side.

'Oh. Hi, Jim, I've been awake since 5.00am, going over things.'

It was obvious that she has been crying again. I was getting very worried about her ability to control her emotions enough to assist in the rescue of the children.

We went for breakfast.

'Is this what the French call a breakfast? I see most of them have a cigarette on at the same time,' she said.

'Yes, it's the way they seem to do things here,' I said.

I was trying to make light conversation with her.

'Jim, a black woman at my work is going to pray for us on Friday afternoon. She and her friends are going to have a prayer meeting in her church. Do you believe in this?'

'Well, yes, Linda, I do. We have right on our side, and if the guv'nor upstairs has been asked for help… we're up and running.'

'Jim, I've been up all night, I haven't slept.'

'You'll be OK.'

'But what if…?'

'We're back to that cat that couldn't piss,' I said, but was thinking, Oh God, give me strength!

We checked out of the hotel and were soon back at Orly. As seems to be the French custom, everyone pushed in front of us as the smell of Gauloises wafted in the air.

'Why can't they queue like everyone else? If this was at home, we would have been screaming at them by now,' Linda said.

However, we were soon on the plane for the sixty-minute flight to Lourdes. Linda just managed to control herself, and on arrival we were met by Winston and Joelle. Joelle immediately took Linda under her wing as we headed off to the hotel, with Winston driving.

The small family hotel was situated in a square in the centre of Lourdes. The family made us welcome, and soon we were in the café that I had visited on many occasions with Winston. The local dentist was there, the 'Irish' Frenchman, and other regulars. The ladies took Joelle and Linda into a corner, where they sat talking.

'So you are the Englishman?' a man asked me.

'Correction, Scottish. You're French?' I asked.

'No, no we're Basque.' he said, gesturing to his friend.

We all laughed.

'So, you are going to get that lady's children home from Spain. Can we help?' he asked.

'Thanks, but most things are taken care of,' I replied.

'We will help you if you need us to do… how do you say

thousand people, where it was likely that everyone knew everyone else. The new car was sure to draw attention, and the worry was that someone associated with scumbag would spot us straight away.

As I was thinking about this we rounded the corner and suddenly I saw the children looking into a field. At the sound of the car, Amanda looked around.

'OK, Linda, they…'

Before I could say anything more, Linda started shouting, 'Jim, Jim, there they are. Quick, get them. Get them.'

She jumped up from behind the seat, still covered in the black cloth.

With my right hand I pushed and held her head down. I started shouting at her. 'Linda get down, get down, don't let them see you.'

'Jim, please don't miss them, please, please!' she shouted.

'Linda, stay down,' I yelled.

I drove past the children. Near to where they where standing was a heap of sand on the dirt track outside a derelict property. An elderly Spanish man was shovelling the sand into a rubber scoop and then carrying it into the house. I slowly drove past the children again while timing the man's routine.

'You've missed them, Jim. You've missed them,' Linda said, sobbing.

'Linda, listen to me. Listen to me carefully. There is a man nearby. As soon as he's gone, we'll get the children. NO, NO!' I said, as she tried to get up again. 'Linda please stay down. And one more favour… Shut Up!'

She started to wail again. It was so distracting; the poor woman was a nervous wreck.

After a final 'Shut up and stay down!' from me, there was silence.

I stopped the car and got out, and as I did I saw that Linda was shaking under the cover. I whispered through the open driver's door, 'Linda, please be very still, and for God's sake don't speak.'

I laid out the map on the bonnet and pretended to scrutinise it. The Spanish worker was now by the sand heap, only fifteen or so feet away, and he was looking at me. It had taken him about thirty seconds to complete his circuit. I nodded to him.

'Hola,' I said, hoping it sounded Spanish.

'Hola,' he replied as he filled the scoop and began walking back to the building. I had thirty seconds.

I walked past the children and Amanda looked at me; she knew what was going on. I prayed: Amanda, please don't shout out. The younger two were looking at the donkeys.

I looked up and down the street; the coast was clear. I walked back past the children and then turned round, 'I'm Jim,' I said, and kept walking.

I quickly looked over my shoulder and saw Amanda grab her sisters by the hand. They started shouting that they wanted to play with the donkeys. I kept walking, ten... twenty feet. I stopped at the car, opened the rear door and stood at the side nearest the boot. The children were three feet from me.

Emma shouted, 'Where are we going Amanda, stop it, I'm going back to the donkeys... please Amanda!'

I held the map up to screen them as they were about to go past.

'Amanda, put your sisters in the car,' I said.

I couldn't believe that she was as calm as can be. She pushed her sisters into the back of the car. I then guided her in, shut the door and casually walked round to the driver's door.

'Mummy, mummy!'

'Darlings,' Linda said.

I reached in and pulled the cover over them. There was much laughing and giggling from below.

'Shush, shush, don't speak, we need to be quiet. Please, darlings, don't make a noise,' Linda said.

'OK, Mummy, OK.'

Then more giggles, getting louder.

The Spanish man came out of the building and looked at me. I held up the map and pointed to my head, curling my index finger against my temple. Getting into the car, I shut and locked the doors.

I began speaking like a second-rate ventriloquist, 'It's OK, he thinks I'm lost. Slowly does it. Please stay under the covers, because anyone looking at the car will only see me.'

There is more laughter and tears from behind me.

'Please, you must all stay down, stay down!' I tried to say this without moving my lips.

I got into the driver's seat and, with my foot ever-so-gently down on the pedal, I eased the car out of Pulgar, round the corner, and then accelerated off.

'Mummy, where are we going? Are we going home?'

'Yes, yes, but be quiet or Jim will shout at us,' Linda said with laughter.

'Mummy, who is Jim?' one of the younger ones asked.

'I'll tell you who Jim is later.'

There was more whispering and giggles from the back as I put down my window and took the 'filo' packages one at a time and placed them on the roof of the car. They gently rolled back and burst as they hit the ground, spreading roofing nails over the road. There were 300 in all - not unlike a little snowstorm, I thought. Anyone following us would have given some business for the local tyre-repair company.

'Mummy, will Daddy find us?' Amanda asked.

'No, no, never,' Linda replied.

I was now driving very fast down the road and soon smelled from the back of the car the unmistakable odour of a child having been sick. I put the windows down and the warm Spanish air flooded in.

'You'll be all right darling. Don't worry, I've got other clothes,' Linda said.

'But Mummy, but mummy…'

'Don't worry, it's not a problem. We will be going on a little plane soon, it's great, you'll love it and then we'll meet Joelle and Winston and then soon after that we will see Grandpa.'

Was this the same Linda who had been shaking in terror a couple of hours earlier in the aircraft?

As I rounded a corner, I dropped my speed instantly. Standing in the road facing me were two Guardia Civil officers with their hands raised in the 'stop' position. I brought the car to a halt.

Linda saw them and said, 'Oh, no! Oh, no! Jim, Jim!'

'OK, OK,' I said. 'All of you sit up; keep laughing; it's a big party. Ditch the cloth on the floor.'

I pulled off the moustache. Emma looked at me in amazement.

'Now listen; if they ask, we're on holiday,' I said.

The two officers walked towards us past their motorcycles at the side of the road. It didn't help that the uniforms made them look like stormtroopers. Did someone see us leave Pulgar with the children? Had the scumbag called them?

They walked slowly towards us and then stopped. One held his arm out. A prison van came out of the field entrance and one officer got onto his motorbike, kick-started it, and accelerated off in front of the van. The other turned round and saluted us before riding in behind the rear of the van.

'OK, OK, we're all OK, don't worry, it's no problem,' I said. 'They were only bringing some prisoners from the fields, they are not interested in us.'

But the children were not really interested in what was going on. They were back to laughing and giggling with Mum.

Joining the main road, I drove as quickly as I dared towards the airport. At a lay-by, I pulled in and we all got out of the car. Linda helped the girls wash their hair and change their clothes. They had looked like urchins from Oliver! I wet and shampooed my hair. The girls had great fun pouring the water over my head.

'Oh, look, he's got black hair,' Maxine said.

Emma looked on in amazement. I used the face cream to remove the glue from my upper lip and then cleaned the number plates with the wipes. I ditched all the clothing, removed the stones from my hat and got back into the car. We were all feeling calmer. The children were eating biscuits and drinking water. Linda was glowing.

Less than an hour later we reached the outskirts of Madrid, where the traffic had started to build up. While waiting for some traffic lights to change, there was suddenly an almighty crash and banging on the roof of the car, which rocked the entire vehicle. Linda and the children went silent and then, after a moment, the children started crying and screaming.

I looked round, 'What the...?'

To my left there was the biggest bull I had ever seen trying to smash its way out of the side of a slatted lorry and across the top of our car.

'Sit tight,' I said.

This was no time to hang around, as the police were running towards us while people were screaming and pointing at the bull. I bumped off the pavement and drove away. Surprisingly, no one seemed to take a blind bit of notice of us or the car. What else could happen, I thought.

When we arrived back at the airport, Nick was waiting outside.

'Hi, this is Nick,' I said.

'Mummy, who is that man?' asked Emma.

'A friend of Jim's.'

'Mummy, who is Jim?'

Nick looked at the car and then at me. He rolled his eyes and shook his head from side to side.

'Jim, a quick word,' he said, as he put his hand on my shoulder and moved me away from the children.

'Yes, Nick,' I said.

'What the fuck happened to the roof?' he asked.

'A bull jumped on it.'

'Bullshit!'

'No, honestly, Nick, it was a bull's hoof.'

'Do you expect me to tell Hertz that a fucking bull jumped on the car? Smith - you're a piss-taker. What happened?'

'Linda, tell Nick what happened,' I said.

Before Linda could speak, there was a little voice from behind her.

'A big cow jumped out of a lorry and the men were hitting it.'

I shrugged my shoulders and held my hands out.

'Would I lie to you, my boy?' I said as he got into the car.

'Cheers, Jim,' Nick shook his head and looked at me. 'Trust an ex-Old Bill to get a kid to verbal for him.'

'Nick, just take it to the Hertz car park, drop it off and then leg it - forget the deposit.'

The last I heard from him he was mumbling, 'A bull jumped onto the car. Bull, my arse.'

We walked hand-in-hand to the immigration counter and produced our passports. The officer casually looked us up and down and waved us through.

The excitement on the plane was electric. The children were laughing and were very, very excited. They were hanging onto their mother and went from tears to laughter and back to more tears, eventually ending up with lots of laughter as Jean-Claude announced, 'Hi, all, we are now in France.'

At touchdown, we were greeted by Winston and Joelle. Then the final part, phoning Bob from a phone box at the airport.

'Hi, Dad, they are with me and Jim,' Linda said. 'We're in France and we are all safe.'

She then started to cry. 'Oh, Dad, we are all safe.'

Emma looked at her, along with the other two. 'Don't cry Mummy, we're with you, please don't cry. Can I speak to Grandpa?'

'Hi, Granddad,' she said.

The conversation appeared to be mostly one-sided from England as Bob spoke to them all.

Finally, I got my chance to get a word in.

'Bob, we are all OK, the children are safe, no dramas. You know what to do when scumbag phones you. We are going back to the hotel and get the children sorted out we'll speak to you later. Everything's fine, no worries, cheers.'

Bob could barely speak as his voice faltered, 'Thanks, Jim, thanks.'

Now for the final piece of the plan.

I'd prepared a script - which we had kept confidential - for Bob to deal with scumbag.

Just after 6.00pm, UK time, scumbag phoned.

'Can I speak to Linda?' he asked.

Bob replied, 'Can I speak to my grandchildren? …What do you mean, the children are having a meal and you had to come to the phone box on your own? You're a no-good, lying bastard. The children are with me and Linda, and they are all now at a friend's house. No, I am not joking, you evil bastard.'

Bob was seriously deviating from my script. He continued, 'No, you can't speak to them. Anyway, I thought you said the children were at your house having a meal. You're a no-good, filthy rotten scumbag. Don't fucking tell me to let you speak to them, you lousy bastard. OK, if you don't believe me, you go and find them in your arsehole of a village.'

Bob, anger and frustration boiling out of him, had waited weeks, if not years, for that conversation.

Meanwhile, we had a meal and then a little celebration in the café before Linda returned to the hotel with the now exhausted children. I remained at the café with Winston. The conversation that night was all about the events of getting the children back. Winston told the story of the bull on the roof of the car to almost every new arrival. I retired at 3.00am.

The next morning at 8.00am I walked carefully into the breakfast room and saw Linda positively glowing with her three little chicks under her wing. Winston and Joelle soon arrived, and we left for the airport and arrived back at Heathrow without any further drama.

Linda and the children received a rapturous reception at Home Farm Close. The children were smothered in kisses, and Bob would not let them out of his sight or grasp. My wife later joined us and we celebrated into the early hours of the morning.

I have often met with the children over the years; they are all fine young ladies now. Every Christmas Eve I would visit with Bob, where the two of us would sit and 'swing the light'. The children would have left presents for me and I for them. It was during one of these occasions that Bob confided in me that scumbag had had plans to sell his two youngest girls into the underground Argentinean sex trade. How he found out about this I never discovered.

Bob had had an amazing life, doing so much for the Spanish people during the Spanish Civil War. It was such a shame that the last Spaniard he met was the scumbag, although he eventually realised, once his anger had subsided, that there were millions of good Spanish people out there.

Unbeknownst to me, during all the drama Bob had been through, he had been suffering from cancer. Too few years after the return of his grandchildren I received a phone call to say that Bob had died. He left a family that he could be proud of.

I went to his funeral, and after the service I sat in the car and watched the three children with their mother walk hand-in-hand from the crematorium. I felt proud at the sight of seeing them together, and sad at the sight of them walking away... I cried.

I miss the Christmas Eve chats with Bob.

The children presented me with a tankard which was engraved with the words: 'Thanks Jim, Love, Linda, Amanda, Maxine and Emma.'

Each Christmas Eve I have a drink from this tankard and think of them all.

Sometimes I see them in Reading, and I am introduced as the man who saved their life. I don't think I did; I just gave it back to them.

As for the scumbag, who cares? What goes around, comes around.

THIRTY-EIGHT

CROWN COURT - A BETTER CURE THAN LOURDES?

After my return home from Spain, it was a real relief to get back to more predicable cases. I was again investigating suspicious insurance claims, work I had done hundreds of times. But, of course, only the doubtful claims were forwarded to me. Each doubtful claim forwarded to me meant keeping the claimants under observation and obtaining video evidence of their activities when possible. When immersed in these, it often seemed as if everyone in the country was suffering from some form of injury sustained at work and seeking compensation of various kinds. That is not to say all these suspect claims were false - out of all of the enquires I undertook over the years, I did find a tiny handful who appeared to be genuine.

It has been said that the law is a blunt instrument (how true!), but occasionally it acts like a rapier, as in the case of the 'postwoman'. She had alleged that she received an injury whilst doing her deliveries. This left her unable to walk without the aid of crutches. The insurers challenged the claim made through her union, and the union responded by taking the case to the High Court.

I kept her under observation for weeks prior to the hearing, capturing her on video as she went shopping, carrying heavy bags home, and generally carrying on a normal life. The day prior to her court appearance, she spent the afternoon shopping in Newport, once again without the use of crutches and walking without difficulty.

When she arrived at court she was assisted out of the taxi by friends, who held her steady as she eased herself onto the crutches and slowly made her way up the steps of the court, with a face distorted in agony.

When her case was called she made her way to the witness box. The judge, on seeing her difficulties, excused her from going into the box and had a chair brought. She slowly positioned herself into the chair, assisted by a court usher who took her crutches and rested them on a table next to her. The court sat in silence as a glass of water was poured for her. She looked up to the usher. 'Thank you,' she whispered in a frail voice.

She then commenced to give her evidence of pain and suffering, testimony that could have brought a tear to a glass eye.

On completion of her evidence the judge asked her if she wished to have a break.

'No, Sir, I'll be okay if I sit still for a few minutes,' she said.

(TAKE 1. Grimace, twist in chair making moaning sounds… Action!)

'Thank you, Sir,' she added.

'Now, are you comfortable enough for the barrister from the insurers to ask you some questions?' the judge asked.

'I think so, Sir'.

Her soft Welsh voice faltered as she replied. A little smile completed the act.

'Very good,' the judge said, as he looked down and nodded to our barrister.

Our barrister rose slowly to his feet, adjusting his wig as he did so.

'I have only two questions for you, Mrs Kilbane.'

He slid his hands onto the lapels of his gown and stared straight at her.

'Are you comfortable?'

(TAKE 2. Further grimace)

'Yes, Sir.'

'That was the first question, and now the second one. Do you know a man called James Smith?'

'No, Sir.'

'Well, Mrs Kilbane, he knows you.'

With that he looked to his left.

'Mr Smith, would you please stand up?'

I stood up.

She looked at me and shrugged.

'Do you recognize him, Mrs Kilbane?'

'No, Sir. I have never seen him in my life, Sir.'

'Well, he knows you, Mrs Kilbane. You see, he has been watching you over the last few months. Not only watching you, but making video recordings of your activities.'

(TAKE 3. Grimace, break into sweat. No acting required.)

'No further questions m'Lud,' said our barrister.

'Call James Smith,' said the Court Usher.

I entered the witness box and commenced my evidence. The video was switched on and was left to run to the end.

Mrs Kilbane stared at the floor, no doubt praying for the ground to open up.

Our barrister rose to his feet.

'Well, Mrs Kilbane, did you recognize anyone in the video?'

Before she could reply the Judge interjected.

'I did.'

The Judge looked at the clock on the wall.

'I think this would be a good time to break for lunch. Before we do, I will wish the court to view this video again and, if possible, I would like any members of the press in the court building to attend. Back at two o'clock.'

'Court will rise,' the Usher said.

After lunch, as soon as the Judge sat down the postwoman's barrister was on his feet.

'Sir, I have spoken to my client during the lunch break and she informs me that she does not wish to pursue this matter.'

The Judge looked down at Mrs Kilbane, ignoring her barrister.

'Perhaps you would like to enter the witness box. Take your

crutches if you wish.'

The video was shown yet again. The local hacks sat furiously writing.

Then Judge Justice Hutchison tore into her.

'There has been startling evidence of exaggeration and deliberate simulation on your part when you walked into this court with an obvious limp.'

The case was immediately dismissed. The Judge gave judgment for the company with costs.

In this case, the evidence saved the insurers a sum of money somewhere in the region of one hundred thousand pounds. Mrs Kilbane had the pleasure of seeing herself exposed as a liar and cheat in the national papers the next day.

Justice, I thought.

On the way home, I stopped off on the motorway for a coffee and to ring the office.

'Anything doing?' I asked my secretary.

'Yes, just a bit! Two guys have got into Winston's house and stuck a gun up his son's nose. You'd better get down there right away.'

FORTY

TRICKY LITTLE BASTARD

During the next couple of months events on the Winston front went quiet and I was back about my usual business. One day when I was out, a man phoned and asked to speak to Winston. My sons Gregory and Steven were home, and Gregory fielded the call. He told him that there was nobody of that name at the house. The caller said he was a friend of Winston, that his car had been stolen and Winston's telephone number had been lost with the theft. He asked Gregory to look in his dad's book for his number. The caller didn't have any luck.

On the back of this, I immediately had all the Skelleys' mail redirected. I would then collect it and send it on, or fly and deliver it personally in Andorra la Vella, where they were staying while their flat was being made ready.

Then, while shopping in Andorra, Joelle's American Express card was declined. I made enquires and discovered that the billing address had been changed to a house in Pyrford, Surrey. The occupant there told me that a man claiming he was Mr Skelley had called to collect his mail, which had wrongly been sent to the Pyrford address. The occupant refused to give it to him and described 'Mr Skelley' as tall and grey-haired with a tanned complexion.

My wife and I went on holiday to Mallorca, where we had met up with Winston and Joelle.

On our return home, a neighbour called over.

'Jim, while you were away, there was a man looking in your

windows. I asked him if I could help, he said it was okay, he was a friend of yours.'

'What did he look like?' I asked.

'Oh, he was tall, long grey hair and well-tanned. Actually, he was rather dishy. He was in a silver Mercedes car. Hold on a minute, I wrote the number down.'

She handed me an envelope with '607 Z 6033' written on it.

Now they were outside my door. I was getting worried, but I tried to pass it off at home as 'no problems'. My wife didn't believe me. In case of a unwelcome visit, I placed cans of oven cleaner strategically around the house.

Soon after I received a telephone call.

'Hello, is that you, Jim?' a male voice asked.

'Yes, who's that?' I replied.

'I'm a friend of Winston, I've been trying to get him at St John's Wood, but there is never any reply on his line.'

'Sorry, what did you say your name was?' I asked.

'Frederick,' he replied.

'Frederick who?'

'Freddie Carter.'

'Sorry, mate, I don't know you. Who exactly are you?' I asked.

'A friend of Winston.'

'I don't have it, and anyway, if I did I, wouldn't give it out to a stranger. Would you really expect me to?'

'No, but it is rather urgent,' he said.

'I guessed it must have been, when you were creeping round my house. Why didn't you drop a line through the letter box?' I said.

'Not me, I've never been to your house.'

'Does '607 Z 6033' mean anything to you, Frank?'

There was a silence for a few seconds. And then, laughingly, he replied, 'What's that "Frank" all about, bloody Neighbourhood Watch?'

'Yes, I suppose so, we also have a neighbourhood photographer. Isn't it time you had a hair cut?' I said.

It was one big bluff. From the description I thought it may be Frank Maple, the alleged brains behind the 1975 £8 million bank robbery on the Bank of America in Mayfair. This was getting scary. I hadn't a clue if the phone call was coming from round the corner and a visit to my home was imminent.

'You tricky little bastard!' he said, and started to laugh.

'You honestly don't think I would give you his details even if I had them,' I said. 'I wouldn't give them to that bent Old Bill who's trying to earn out of this. At least you've been up front. I'm prepared to have a meet with you, but I can't give you anything. Not even for an "earner", before you offer it.'

'Okay, do me one favour. If you do speak to him, tell him we want our money,' he said.

'Okay,' I replied, and with that the line went dead.

I walked back into the lounge. My wife looked up.

'Who was that? she asked.

'Only some guy wanting Winston to get in touch, no problems.'

'I don't want them coming round here looking for him. Anyway, how did they get this number?'

'I fancy they got it from Judas, anyway they won't come here, I said.

Three minutes later the door bell rang.

'Hi, Jim, is Janet in?' asked our next door neighbour. 'You can come round and do mine when you're finished'

'Sorry?' I said.

She nodded to the oven spray canister in my hand. I had subconsciously picked it up before I opened the door.

'You should wear rubber gloves when you use that stuff, it can be dangerous.'

I never again used my house or office phone to contact Winston.

The time came for the Skelleys to move into their new apartment. I hired a lorry and loaded their possessions, and together with Dave, a former RAF-trained 'expert in map reading', set off to Dover to catch the first morning Hovercraft to Calais.

At 5.30am I was in an import/export agent's office getting the documents stamped. I walked out of the office, into the arms of Judas. He seemed shocked that I had seen him, and for once was tongue-tied.

'Oh, hi, Jock, what brings you here?' he asked.

'Funnily enough, I was just going to ask you that.'

'Em, I'm just waiting for a load of bent gear that is coming in from abroad. And you?'

'Just going over to Calais for some shopping,' I said.

'What, with a four-tonner?'

By his very statement he tipped that he had been watching for my arrival.

'Will Winston be there?' he asked.

'No chance. Must go,' I replied.

Fortunately, I had shown on the paper work that the goods were to be delivered to Joelle's mother's house in Lourdes.

We set off. I was not happy. Judas being in Dover at 5.00am to collect bent gear from abroad? He was there to get a look at my manifest. Had Judas got prior notice of our sailing time and passed it on to his 'friends'?

We boarded the Hovercraft and soon set off, but not before I had noted the registration numbers of every car on board. In Calais, my map-reading expert successfully got us off the Hovercraft. But we had only gone about a mile when he insisted that we should turn right and, despite my protests, he again insisted that the map was correct. I was directed up a three-hundred-yard-long cul-de-sac. The air turned blue as I reversed the truck back down the street with cars parked either side. Not the best of starts.

FORTY-ONE
ANDORRA

Three days later we arrived in Andorra la Vella, the capital of the Principality, and unloaded the family's property to the third floor penthouse flat.

Prior to leaving I had undertaken an enquiry from a new client in Andorra. I carried out the enquiry on his behalf. I forwarded my report and invoice to him, but despite reminders he didn't reply and I didn't receive my fees.

On the first Sunday morning in town I went to his large detached house on the mountainside. Electric security gates controlled the entrance to the spacious grounds.

I rang the entry phone.

'Mr Smith for Mr Stein,' I said.

'I'm sorry, master not in, he back later,' a woman's voice replied.

'When will he be home?' I asked.

'Moment.'

The line went dead. A small Filipina walked down the drive and stopped about six feet from the gates.

'I so sorry, I no hear you properly,' she said.

'That's okay; I would like to speak to Mr Stein if possible. Yes?'

'No, he will be home, tree hours. You understand?'

'Is he your husband?' I asked.

She burst in to a state of uncontrollable giggling.

Dave answered for her, 'No, me only here for scwooing!'

She didn't hear him as she continued her giggling between big

281

intakes of breath. I fully expected her to have an asthma attack any second.

'No! Me only maid. He no wife.'

'I told you, only for scwooing.' Dave was at it again.

Despite my best efforts, I burst out laughing, followed by the maid and Dave.

'Your friend very funny man,' she said.

'Yes, very funny man, you should see him at map reading. Okay, you give him this and tell him Jim Smith has arrived from Reading. I'm in the Palace Hotel. I will await his call, thank you.'

The next morning I received a call from Stein.

'Good morning old boy, how are you, got my long-awaited report?'

'Yes, I'll see you in the Rotunda café in one hour,' I said.

'Superb, the Rotunda in one hour. Bye for now.'

I sat at one table and Dave at another.

A little, bald Jewish man walked into the café. He was dressed in very expensive casual clothes and white handmade shoes. A designer gold watch hung loosely on his wrist.

'Ah, you must be Jim,' he said.

'Yes, that's me.'

We shook hands. He had conman written all over him and spoke with, as they say in Glasgow, 'jorries' (marbles) in his mooth (mouth).

'I've been very anxious to receive your report.'

'So anxious, you didn't think to call me and ask where it was,' I said.

'I knew you would be an extremely busy and I just thought, it will arrive when the chap's ready.'

We had a few coffees with brandy. His tongue gradually loosened. What twenty minutes before had been 'superb and jolly good show' was now 'spot on and kosher'. I looked at him. It soon became obvious from what he was saying that he had read my report.

'You were trying to have me over, and unless your little flat-faced friend back at your house nicked it, you got my report. Correct?' I said.

'I've been so busy recently, and I must admit, I didn't expect you to come all this way to collect.'

'Well, here I am, and I'm here to collect.'

'Is a cheque okay?' he asked.

'Now, what do you think?' I asked.

'You are a very brave man to have come all this way on your own and expect to be paid in cash.'

'Yeah! That's what I thought, so I brought a mate - or in your other language, a chum,' I said.

I looked over at Dave and smiled. Dave smiled back and gave a little wave by raising his right hand and wiggling his fingers.

'Tell me one thing. Is that your truck with "Adrian Reading" on the side?' Stein asked.

'Yes.'

'Why on earth did you drive down in that?

'Oh, just in case we had to take you back to England to collect my fees,' I said.

He did not reply. We walked the short distance to the bank, I collected my fees in pesetas and left Mr Stein standing on the footway.

'You know, Dave, he thought he could scwoo me!' I said.

FORTY-TWO
PARCELLED UP!

After my return to the UK, I had not heard from Winston for a couple weeks. One evening after work I was at home watching television when the telephone rang. My wife answered it.

'It's Winston for you.'

'Hi, long time no hear. How are you?' I asked.

'Not good, we were parcelled up,' Winston replied.

I had never heard the expression before.

'What do you mean 'parcelled up'?'

'Kidnapped. They had us out of Andorra and we're now in Fuengirola, in the Costa del Sol.'

'Are you both okay?' I asked.

'Yes, I'm in the police station at the moment. We've living in a little villa in the Avenue Argentina, just behind the nick. We've got an armed police guard at the back and front of the house. Can you get down here tomorrow?'

'Yes, I'll see you tomorrow,' I said.

I walked back into the living room my wife looked at me.

'What's wrong?' she asked.

'Winston and Joelle were kidnapped. It's okay, they're safe in the Costa del Sol. I'm off there tomorrow.'

'Be very careful,' she said with a worried expression.

Janet was growing more concerned as the Winston saga went on, and who could blame her. She never once throughout our married life attempted to stop me going about my chosen career, although on a number of occasions asked me, 'Why don't you become a milkman?' She knew it was in my blood, and that I could not change.

At 7.00pm the following day my flight touched down at Malaga airport. I disembarked, and was greeted by the warm perfumed air that says 'welcome to Spain'. Making my way to arrivals, I was met by Winston and Pedro Parria, the local chief of the CID. Two of his officers stood about ten feet away, watching the people in the lounge. They then escorted us to Winston's Rolls Royce, which had yet another police officer standing guard over it. The car had Monaco number plates, and was the one used by Prince Charles and Princess Diana when they visited Monaco.

After about an hour's drive with our police escort we arrived at Fuengirola Police Station, and went directly to Pedro's office. He and I had a private meeting, where he quizzed me about both Winston's and my background. He seemed satisfied with my answers. We then adjourned to another room, where the desks were stacked with documents, false UK passports and photographs from houses the police had raided in connection with Winston's abduction. Winston joined us and we went through the events leading up to the Skelleys' unscheduled arrival in Spain.

Winston began.

'It was on the 19th of October, and Joelle and I had been out for dinner the night before and returned home about 11.00pm. Sometime in the early morning Joelle heard someone at the door, and instead of using the spy hole, she opened the door. On the landing there were four guys, they were all wearing surgical gloves and carrying guns. I was out cold and hadn't a clue what was going on. They pinned Joelle against the wall in the hallway and held a pistol against her head. They told her to keep her mouth shut, and then one of them came for me. I was awakened as a gun was held against my head. I got up and put my robe on. Then the other three came in with Joelle. The men were Frank Maple, Peter Simms, James Marsden and Neil Robertson. You know of Robertson, Jim, he was the one that wanted to invest £600K a couple of years back. They threatened if I didn't do what I was told they would take us into the mountains and kill us. They made it quite clear that our bodies would never be found. After tearing the place apart to get all my bank statements, they started to count how much money I had and said they were going to have the lot. We sat for hours waiting for banking business to start. I was then made to phone one of my banks to transfer £57,000 from one of my accounts to another of their team in Zurich. About midday three of them left, leaving me with Robertson. When they were leaving they showed me photographs of my sons, Richard and Philip. They even showed us pictures of Joelle's mother and my ex-wife and told us where they ate, where they did their shopping, etc. They knew every bloody thing, and as they went out the door they warned us in no uncertain terms what would happen to the families if I did not cooperate. Oh, and by the way, they knew all about you, they called you the "tricky little bastard".'

'Oh, well they were half right, I said. I've got a birth and marriage certificate with both my parents names on it.'

An officer translated what I had said to Pedro, and he smiled as he lit up yet another cigarette.

'How on earth did they trace you to your flat?' I asked Winston.

Winston looked at me sheepishly.

'I made a phone call to Judas to see if he had any information for me. He said he was rushing out of the office to do a job and would call me back as soon as he came back in. Without thinking I gave him my phone number.'

'Winston, please don't tell me you gave your number to Judas.' I said.

He looked at the floor and nodded, then continued.

'It was a couple of days later, when he called back and said it was a bit iffy talking on the phone and suggested it would be better if he came and saw me. That bastard has sold me down the river.'

Joelle sat shaking her head.

'Jim, he could have had both of us killed. I told Winston, listen to Jim, have nothing to do with that man. Oh well, we all make mistakes, I should never have opened that door. Sorry.' She reached over and took Winston's hand.

Winston continued.

'Robertson stayed with us for five days, and on the Monday

night he took two-and-a-half grand from me and stuffed it into his pocket. He then looked at me and Joelle and said, "Get your gear, we're going for a trip." He took us downstairs to the Roller and drove us to the Don Pepe Hotel in the Marbella. It's a five-star job. They had booked a room for us. When we went to our room, Maple and Simms were waiting for us. They kept us there for two days and then moved us to a villa in Puerto Banus, a few miles up the road. They let us sleep there, and when we woke up the next morning they were gone. We took off in a taxi to Malaga airport and flew to Lourdes, where we went to Joelle's mother's house.'

'Joelle's mother said a man called Frank had phoned and would phone back in a short time. The call came, it was Maple. He said "If you want to see you sons alive again, you will do what you're told." I was instructed to get to Ibiza the next day. Believe me, I went because these guys were deadly serious. In Ibiza I was met by Maple and Simms. The gang had discovered I had another £92,700 in the Handelsbank in Zurich, and they were convinced I had funds in other banks.'

'I was then taken back to somewhere in Fuengirola, where they put me in a villa. By now, I hadn't a clue where I was, I could only see out of a small barred-window. I was convinced they were going to kill me. I put my fingerprints all over the place, I even pulled hair out of my toupee and put it down the sink for the Police to find. Then they made me sign over my yacht, the Patrallis, which they got £86,000 for, and then my Roller, which they sold for £30,000. During this time, Robertson and Maple flew to Zurich to collect the 92 grand. Something went wrong; they began to panic and then moved me to a villa up near Mijas belonging to a man called Steven Riscovitch. I was convinced this was the end. I had even hid my sleeping tablets inside my underpants in case they made me swallow them to make it look like suicide.'

I interrupted, 'Did you say Steven Riscovitch? What did he look like?'

Winston described him.

'I think this man's correct name is Steven Rich,' I said. 'I photographed him years ago when I was in the Police. He is a bank robber.'

This was translated for Pedro, and he nodded and smiled, saying, 'Do you not have prisons in England?'

Winston continued.

'They wanted me to make another phone call to my bank. I got the impression there was some problem, and for some reason they did not want to use the house phone. One of them put me on the back of his motorcycle with my hands tied. He took me along the Mijas road where he stopped at a phone box. All the way to the phone box I had been looking for an opportunity to jump off, but it wasn't possible with my hands tied. Besides, it's a country road with no place to go.

'He took a bag with a load of coins and we walked to the phone box. He put in loads of money and telephoned my bank. Just as I started to speak to the bank manager, he walked over to the bike to get a cigarette. As soon as his back was to me, I hung up and immediately called Joelle and gave her my rough location. When he turned round and walked back towards me, I pretended to be talking to the bank. I signed to him for a cigarette and he gave me the one he had, walking back to the bike for another.

'The bike was only about six feet away. I didn't even think, I dropped the phone and ran. I jumped over a small wall and fell, bouncing down a slope. I could hear him shouting and screaming at me as I hit some concrete, and then somehow got onto my knees. When I looked up there was a man coming through one of those screen things - you know the type, they're all beads. He was dressed in chef's whites, and as I ran past him into a kitchen I started shouting for the police. The staff looked at me as if I was deranged; I thought they were going to throw me out. Then one of them saw my hands were tied. It all calmed down and he cut my hands free. They gave me some water and I started sobbing like a baby. Then the police arrived and brought me here.'

Pedro looked at his watch. It was now 10.00pm and time for supper. We left the office and walked down the twisting staircase and into the parking area where the Roller waited. We drove to a Tapas bar in The Avenue de Mijas in Fuengirola. As we pulled up, I felt as if I was back in Glasgow. The bar was on the ground floor of what appeared to be a tenement. It was without doubt one of the best, if not the best tapas bar in the area. Then again, would the Old Bill from whatever country take 'a cock' to a rubbish place! I have been there many times since and the standard is still as high.

Later that night, I went with the Spanish Police as they raided the homes of various UK exiles, and more correspondence between London's top criminals and their 'friends' in Spain was recovered. I couldn't believe how careless they had been in keeping this evidence, as it was to prove invaluable to the Metropolitan Police in London.

FORTY-THREE
BUENO BANDIDOS

The following morning, Winston and I were back in the police station with Pedro and his team. We looked over some of the photographs and documents that had been removed from the raided properties. It was an Aladdin's cave of information for the UK police. Had I not have been attached to C11, I doubt if the faces in the photographs would have meant anything to me other than the odd TV personality who had found himself photographed with the top echelons of the British criminal fraternity.

I telephoned DS John French at Scotland Yard.

'John, I'm in a nick in Spain. I'm doing a job down here, I don't suppose you can pop over.'

'Yes, I'm packing my bags as we speak… you have got to be joking,' he replied.

I relayed all the information I had and he asked when I'd be back in the UK.

'In a few days,' I replied, 'I'll give you a ring tomorrow. There is so much information that we've found. That Jimmy Jeffries is down here, and it looks as if Freddie Foreman and the Knights are in town.'

Unknown to me at that time, the Knight Brothers - Ronnie and John - along with Freddie Foreman, a vicious and self-confessed murderer, were suspected of being involved in a £59.5 million robbery a few months earlier on the London Headquarters of Security Express. They would all subsequently arrested and convicted as a result of the documents seized in Spain.

'Your friend knows Mr Jeffries?' Pedro had overheard my conversation.

'Yes, a few years ago John was taking washing to a launderette. He saw Jeffries and another man watching a security van doing a delivery to a bank in the east side of London. Two weeks later the bank was robbed of thousands of pounds and later, as a result of John's evidence and what he had seen from the launderette, the gang was arrested.'

'London is a very large place, how did he manage to see him?' Pedro asked.

'John has a memory like a computer,' I replied. 'He knows hundreds of good criminals by sight. A few years ago, one of Jeffries' friends, a bank robber, had been given a good hiding and was taken to hospital. John saw Jeffries visiting him, and remembered Jeffries' face from when he had last seen him ten years before.'

'Jim, when you say the man was "good hiding", where was he hiding?'

'No, no, he had been beaten up, hit, attacked.'

The officer looked puzzled.

'And so, a good criminal, is he good?'

'Em, well, no. He is a professional criminal. He plans all the jobs before he does them and then steals property worth lots of money; it's slang, understand?'

'I think so. Bueno Bandidos! Correct?'

'Correct!'

We went into the adjoining room and started to look through the paperwork. The Spanish Police had recovered thousands of documents which I knew would be invaluable to the British police. It was a virtual Who's Who of the UK's top criminals, complete with photographs and telephone numbers. There was even the days and times when to telephone 'safe' phone boxes in the UK. I would not be exaggerating if I said there was in excess of two thousand pieces of information. It was imperative that this material went into the correct hands in England.

The remainder of the morning was spent going through the

evidence. No sooner did we think we were reaching the end of the task than another load was carried in and dumped in front of Winston and myself.

'Muchas bueno Bandidos,' said one of the Spanish officers with a laugh. A little bit of 'Met language' had been introduced to Spain.

I left the Police station and walked to the town centre. At the Plaza de la Constitucion I sat outside a café opposite the large white-washed church of The Virgin of the Rosary. I was watching the world go by, taking in the sunshine and thoroughly enjoying the atmosphere, when I heard 'You're 'avin a bleedin' laugh, she's an old slapper, the bike of bleedin' Bermondsey.'

I couldn't catch any more of the Londoner's 'slag' accent as he walked across the square and into a bar on the opposite side - the London Bar. How could I have missed it! Crossing the square to another café near the London Bar, I sat sipping my San Miguel and watching the clientele go in and out. Seeing their faces was like attending an open day at Parkhurst Prison. I had covertly photographed most of them over the past years. The difference now was they were bronzed, with their gold jewellery glistening in the sun. However, they still walked the same way and had the same mannerisms. As it is said, you can take the man out of Bermondsey, but you can't take Bermondsey out of the man.

As I sat watching these people living the life of Riley, I kept thinking of the bent cops who over the years had helped them to where they were now: A handful of so-called police officers who had taken money from these people; the so-called police officers who would not have had the bottle to do a bank job or similar robbery, but were prepared to 'ponce' off the robbers who had; the so-called police officers who allowed criminals to walk free for 'a drink'. Some police officers had even gone on holiday with criminals and were even stupid enough to be photographed with them. My thoughts then turned to the hundreds of thousands of honest officers and a police force that had been tarnished by this handful. A tarnish that would take years to remove.

I left the café and made my way back to the Police station to continue my search through the paperwork with Winston and the Spanish police officers. More contact details kept appearing, including the address in Pyrford, Surrey where the Skelleys' American Express card statement had been redirected to. Our next find was a shoe-box sized cache of forged £50 notes.

As I looked through the photographs, one jumped out at me. It was a picture of some criminals leaning against a silver Mercedes, registration 607 Z 6033 - the one that had been outside my house. Other pictures showed robbers leaning against an American car parked outside a very expensive house in Florida. The photograph showed the car registration number and the name of the boulevard where one of the robbers lived. It was Mickey Green.

Michael John Paul Green was the mastermind behind a robbery at Barclay's Bank in Ilford in Essex, the very bank job that John had seen Jeffries planning. Green was jailed for eighteen years for his part in that robbery, where £237,000 was stolen, a very large sum of money in 1970. Green was named by a supergrass as the leader of what was known as the 'Wembley Mob', a gang of bank robbers who stole somewhere in the region of 1.5 million pounds over four years. Another photograph showed him at his luxury villa in the Costa del Sol. This in itself was a major breakthrough in tracing this armed robber and drug dealer, who over the next few years evaded arrest as he fled around the world including the USA, where under a false name he rented Rod Stewart's luxury home.

I kept in touch with John French at the Yard while I was going through the documents. Typical of him, he logged everything in his little red books and kept everything to himself until I returned.

A name that kept appearing was 'Casa Bermuda', a house situated just off the Carretera de Fuengirola, the mountain road between the coast and the beautiful 'white' village of Mijas. I took a bus ride to Mijas and walked back down the road looking for the house. After about a mile I found it, situated on the left hand side of the road. It's double wooden gates with a security entry system kept any prying eyes away.

Later that evening I returned to the area and approached it from the rear. I crept through the shrubland to as close to the villa as I dared to go. The noise of dogs barking and the constant chirping of crickets were the only sounds. I lay still, looking at the grounds with a luxurious floodlit swimming pool rippling as a waterfall trickled into it. A barbeque had been lit and the smoke spiralled upwards into the starlit sky. The still of the evening was disturbed by the sound of the wooden gates opening and a car being driven up the slope to the gravel parking area. The gates automatically closed behind the vehicle.

The car, a top of the range Mercedes convertible, pulled up. Two men opened the doors and got out. Sitting on the rear coachwork with their feet on the rear seats were two females. The driver and his friend took them by the waist and lifted the giggling occupants out.

Another couple came out of the house, wine glasses in their hands. He was dressed in white trousers, white shoes and a floral shirt. She had some form of silk robe covering a bikini. The open robe flowed behind her as she glided onto the patio. The scene could have been from a classic film. I started to think it was time to get out of there, I'd got the wrong house.

The bell from the Mijas church echoed down the valley. The scent of bougainvillea wafted through the still air. It was an idyllic location, a million miles from the hustle and bustle of London. I soaked it in, Heaven!

'Get you bleedin' 'ands off me arse.'

The shrill voice of one of the ladies rang out, followed by a burst of high-pitched laughter drowning out the melodic church bell.

'You saucy git, what do you fink I am?'

She let out a scream, followed by, in their words, 'a gob full' of obscenities.

I was too close to a London 'team' and I wasn't invited to the barbeque. The only thing they would have served up to me if they had found me was a good hiding or worse. I crept out of the area and walked the four miles back to the police station.

Our activities in Spain resulted in a number of people being arrested and charged with extortion and kidnapping. These included Robertson, Jeffries, Rich and a man called Michael Reilly. Wanted notices were issued for Maple, Simms, Marsden and Michael Green. At a preliminary court hearing, some of Winston's money was returned to him.

I returned to London, and during a series of meetings with John French we went over the evidence I had brought from the

Spanish police, including a sample of forged currency, a number of photographs and numerous names and addresses.

A few days later I had a meeting with Commander Trevor Lloyd-Hughes and related the whole story to him.

'There is only one thing for it, Jim, put a report into the ACC (Assistant Commissioner Crime) and deliver it by hand to his office,' he said.

'How do you fancy a trip down to Spain, Trevor?' I asked.

'I would love to, but I doubt if they will let me off division to go. Make sure you take 'Frenchie' with you. Let me know how you get on. You don't give up, do you? You should never have left the Job. It's a different Job now, we got rid of the villains at the top, but it will take a long time, if ever, to get our good name back.'

I prepared my report and took it to the front hallway at New Scotland Yard. After a few minutes, a woman arrived and spoke to the PC at the desk. He pointed at me and she walked over, 'Mr Smith?' she asked.

'Yes, Jim Smith.' I replied.

'I'm Mr Kelland's Secretary, I believe you have a letter for Mr Kelland.'

I handed it to her. She thanked me and walked me to the exit, and shook my hand and I left.

As I walked away I thought to myself. I never gave anyone my name before she arrived, and yet she knew mine. Trevor had been in touch.

My letter read:

G J Kelland
Assistant Commissioner Crime
New Scotland Yard London

7th November 1983

Dear Sir,

I am a former Metropolitan Police Officer, having served a period of 13 years. Over the past year I have been carrying out inquiries on the behalf of a Winston Robert Skelley, who is currently wanted on warrant. Skelley states that he has an answer to the allegation and intends to plead not guilty. I know very little about this matter.

I was employed by Skelley to trace suspects involved in the gold bullion (VAT) fraud. Skelley is currently in Spain and was recently kidnapped by a number of London criminals. He was held for a period of seven days, during which time the people involved drained his bank accounts of all funds. There seems very little doubt their intention was to kill him. He escaped and a number of British subjects are in custody in Spain.

Over the past year, Skelley has shown to me a desire to inform police of various criminal matters, but has been afraid to do so due to his fear of corruption in the Police Force.

On his release in Spain I visited him and, together with the Spanish Police, examined numerous documents which relate to criminals who are without doubt involved in serious crime. Skelley, at my instigation, has agreed to meet any police officer that I nominate and could guarantee their honesty and integrity. Having worked with Commander Trevor Lloyd-Hughes and Detective Sergeant John French (C11), I had no hesitation in stating that these officers were of this calibre.

May I ask you to seriously consider allowing these officers to go to Spain with myself and interview Skelley, who is prepared to put all this information on paper. Inspector Parria of Grupo Local Policia Judicial at Fuengirola and Kingsley Knapley (Skelley's solicitor) are aware of this request. I feel if this is done it will result in a major breakthrough in organized crime within this country and the USA.

FORTY-FOUR
THE CHOCOLATE SHOP

Five days later I was on a flight to Malaga with Commander Phillip Corbett and 'Frenchie'. Phil was the officer in charge of C11, and I had known him for years. He was an honest man about whom I had never heard a bad word said, and I was very pleased that he had been chosen.

At Malaga Airport we were greeted by Winston, who drove us to Fuengirola Police Station in his Rolls Royce; after all, if it was good enough for the Prince of Wales and Princess Diana, it was good enough for 'the Commander and Frenchie!'

Pedro, together with a translator, ushered the two of them to his office at the police station, while Winston and I sat in the canteen sipping coffee. No doubt the Spanish Police were going to check me out with the Met Police. I would not have expected anything less. After about an hour they returned to the canteen and joined us. It appeared I had passed the test. I later discovered Dilley had not dared put anything detrimental on my records.

We then drove John to the Piramides Hotel, where he dropped off the luggage and returned to the 'nick' and the four of us started to scrutinize the documents. We were like children in a chocolate shop, as it appeared that almost every piece of paper, letter, or photograph held a wealth of information about criminal activities unknown to C11. I went to the local photographers and bought his entire stock of film. My trusty Pentax camera was put to good use, as over the next few days everything was copied and handed over to John for processing at the Yard.

We then went on a sightseeing tour of the various properties purchased with the proceeds of crime. These included luxury villas, flats, business properties, restaurants, plots of lands and nightclubs in Puerto Banus, one of the most expensive areas in Spain.

On Saturday, 26th November 1983 we were sitting in the lounge of the Piramides Hotel having coffee. John was suffering from writer's cramp, having taken a forty-eight page statement from Winston over the previous few days.

Phillip Corbett wanted to phone back to the Yard.

'You can use the house phone over there, Maria will connect you,' I said, pointing to the telephonist sitting behind a glass screen opposite two pine telephone boxes situated in the corner of the foyer.

We sat drinking our coffees. Time passed, we ordered more coffees. John looked up and said, 'He's taking his time, you don't reckon the doors are jammed?'

'No, he is phoning in your expenses, John,' I replied.

As I said this, Mr Corbett emerged from the kiosk struggling with its folding doors, which had not seen any maintenance for some time. He was reading some notes he had just written.

'Everything okay, Guv?' John asked.

'Not really. A team has just turned over a warehouse at London airport. They have had tons of gold away. Apparently, it goes into many millions of pounds. It must be bad as they have got Powis out of his bed, and he in turn has got Gilbert Kelland out of his.'

David Powis was an Assistant Commissioner Crime, a head of all detectives in the Met. Gilbert Kelland was also an Assistant Commissioner. This was to turn out to be the biggest robbery at that time in British history and became known as the Brink's-Mat job.

We returned to the Police station and discussed the matter with Pedro.

'How many pounds did they take?' he asked.

'We can't be sure, but it will be millions,' Phillip replied.

'Phillip, can I help?' Pedro asked.

'I will have to phone London and get more information, may

I use your phone?'

Pedro pushed his phone across the desk, saying, 'I will take Jim and Winston for coffee.'

Pedro knew Phillip wanted privacy. We had our coffee and upon returning Mr Corbett was finishing his call.

'Phillip, I've been thinking, would it help you if we heard what some British people in town are talking about?' Pedro asked.

'Yes, that would be very helpful, who were you thinking of?'

'We have seen many British here who seem to have lots of money but do not appear to be good people, do you understand? The Cuerpo Superior de Policia, the Branch that deals with detective work has set up a department in Malaga, called the International Delinquency Squad to look into the activities of foreign nationals. If it helps you, I will tell you what these people are talking about later this afternoon.'

We left and had lunch. Not a 'Met type', forty-five minute canteen break. This was a Spanish grub break that lasted at least two hours and was complemented with a couple of bottles of wine. Naturally, this was followed by a siesta. We met back at the Police station at 7.00pm.

'Phillip, the British people have been very busy talking to each other about your robbery. Here, these are for you.'

And with that he produced a number of audiotapes from his desk drawer and put one into a tape recorder. It started with the ringing of a telephone, which was answered by a male with a cockney accent.

'Fuck me, have you heard the news?' said the caller.

'Yes, bleedin' Brink's-Mat, what a tickle.'

'That should keep the Old Bill busy and keep the edge off us.'

Six months before the Brink's-Mat job, £6 million had been stolen in a raid on Security Depot in East London. Was 'Keep the edge off us' significant?

Pedro stopped the tape.

'Will this help you?'

'I am sure it will. Thank you very much,' Phillip said.

Then Pedro, with a twinkle in his eye, looked at Mr Corbett.

'And now I need a favour.'

'If I can I will help,' replied Phillip.

'If we give you Torremolinos, will you give us Gibraltar?' asked Pedro.

A few days after, John and Mr Corbett returned to the UK, as did I. I didn't get to listen to the rest of the tapes, and although I would have liked to, I just didn't think it was the correct thing to do.

As a result of my report to the Mr Kelland, a few months later Britain applied for permission for two Metropolitan Police officers to work in Malaga. With the wealth of information taken back to the UK by Detective Sergeant John French and his boss Commander Phillip Corbett, this was approved. It soon became clear that the information was so good that a further twelve officers were sent down to assist in what was a very secret operation.

What happened since has been well documented. Numerous criminals were arrested and returned to the UK. Freddie Foreman, one of the men wanted for the Security Express job, was arrested as he sunbathed in shorts and a tee shirt on the Costa del Sol, and brought back to England. Another bank robber, Ronnie Knight, the former husband of the actress Barbara Windsor, was subsequently arrested for his part in the same robbery and served a considerable time in prison.

The end of my involvement in the Spanish affair also marked the end of my close association with Winston. The irony about the gold saga was that the villains believed Winston had stolen their money, which they had stolen from the UK Government. If that was the case, that very same money paid the fees that I had received from Winston and thus circuitously led to the arrest of so many criminals. Oh, well, money is made to go round!

Where did the money go?

I don't fully know, but in one case a café owner's daughter in Lourdes was involved in a very bad traffic accident where she had sustained serious injuries to her face after going through the windscreen of the car. There was no hospital in the area that could adequately treat her. Winston had her flown by a private air ambulance to a top hospital in Paris. He picked up the bill for the flights and all of her treatment.

I liked Winston, Joelle and their family. He was honest with me and always settled my accounts.

As so often happens when an investigation reaches its conclusion, I lost contact with the client. Some years later, when my wife and I were on a cruise in the Mediterranean, we met up with Joelle in Ibiza where she informed us of Winston's death.

A few years before, a client had gone to visit him on his yacht. On the completion of their business, they walked to a local café. Winston complained of feeling unwell and asked the client to drive him to the local hospital. At the front door of the hospital he had a massive heart attack and died.

During 1987, Phil Corbett and John French retired from the Police. I attended Mr Corbett's farewell dinner, where he was awarded his Commander's sword and was praised by police officers from all over the world, in particular his work for the FBI. At the end of the evening he took me to one side and thanked me for all my work in Spain: 'If it hadn't been for you and what you did, Spain would never have opened up so soon.'

I too was rewarded by the Metropolitan Police, or rather by one of their officers, Sgt. John French, who bought me a C11 Tie.

Oh, well, as I have said before, 'informants fees' take some time to be approved. Perhaps after twenty-five years the papers have been lost.

However, if you are reading my book, my reward will be that it has been passed for publication.

FORTY-FIVE

LOOKING FORWARD TO RETIREMENT

Things were looking good. I had plenty of work coming in and my wife, Janet, had reached a senior position within Hewlett Packard. It was a demanding job, but with the support and respect of her team, she was coping well. She was a strong woman and was well thought of in the organization. However, as many in industry admit, certain males have a hatred of women being promoted above them.

Such was the case of two managers in France and Holland. They made her life so difficult that she took early retirement in 2003. With our new-found freedom, we were having a great time cruising and holidaying.

About eighteen months after leaving she received a phone call from Hewlett Packard.

'HP want me back as a contractor,' she announced. I always knew Janet felt that she had not fulfilled her potential there, and we both agreed that she should return. This was an enjoyable time for her, as she was able to work with former colleagues and advise on contracts worth tens of millions of pounds.

A few months later she was complaining of feeling unwell, coupled with suffering from halitosis. Visits were made to the doctor, who suggested off-the-shelf medicines and a visit to the dentist. Also, there was noticeable swelling in her abdominal area. Her conditions did not improve. Eventually, her doctor sent her to the Royal Berkshire Hospital in Reading for further examinations, but the results of these tests were negative.

In November 2005, with Janet still suffering from the same symptoms, we again attended the Royal Berkshire Hospital where she underwent an internal examination. The consultant sat us down and showed us two small Polaroid pictures. 'This is your insides, where there is a small polyp,' he indicated this with his pen. 'It's nothing to worry about, we'll send it off for tests. There is a small amount of 'poo' stopping the camera going round the corner. However, I can assure you there is no cancer in your body. Go home have a drink and a nice meal.'

Janet continued to work and did regular exercise at the gym. A couple of weeks later she telephoned from work and told me she was coming home as she felt terrible. I drove her directly to the Royal Berkshire, where the doctors now realized there was 'something not right'.

The guesswork continued until a young doctor suggested a basic X-ray. The results of this came back as showing an internal blockage. She would have to stay in for further tests.

Two days later, she underwent major surgery. I was with her in the recovery room as she came round and was joking with the nurses as to how the X-Factor was getting on.

A doctor took me to a private room.

'Your wife's got cancer, it's all over the place. Mr Farouk has removed some of it, but she's only got a twenty-five percent chance of recovery.'

I sat in silence, my ears were hissing. Cancer? Twenty-five percent?

She was in the gym four nights ago... no, he's got it wrong. I was in another world, everything was fuzzy. It may sound silly, but to me this was like swimming underwater.

I sort of surfaced, out of this non-existent pool. The doctor was still there staring at me, his lips were moving but I couldn't hear anything. Suddenly, as if a radio had been re-adjusted and had clicked on to the correct station, sound came out.

'So, as I was saying it's a twenty-five percent of recovery. Do you want me to tell her or will you do it?' he asked.

'No, not you, eh, I... em. I just can't think straight,' I said. 'What about the surgeon who did the operation?'

'Yes, that's an idea. He can answer any questions she may have. He'll be back to work on Monday.'

I went back to Janet's bed, the screens were drawn. I parted a small gap, quietly made my way in and walked over to the side of the bed. She looked so peaceful lying there sleeping, as if without a care in the world. I held her hand as the tears ran down my face.

Our oldest son Gregory was in Spain with his fiancée, Nicki. His brother, Steven, was at work, where I telephoned him. He drove straight to the hospital. Later, we sat in my car, sobbing our hearts out.

I telephoned my sister Catherine in Edinburgh and broke the news to her. She flew down at once. I called Janet's brother, Hugh Murray, a dentist in Edinburgh who in turn contacted his brother George, a retired teacher in Troon, Ayrshire. Disturbingly, throughout her long illness neither of them visited her.

On the Monday, Mr Farouk sat and broke the bad news to Janet. He had a wonderful bedside manner and our family will never forget all he did, both at the bedside and in the operating theatre, when others were ready to give up. Gregory, Nicki, Catherine, Steven and his girlfriend and myself later stood in a corridor outside Janet's room in shock and in tears.

Due to inadequate, not to say disgusting, aftercare in the Kennet Ward, we moved Janet to the Capio Hospital in Reading, where the attention she received there resulted in her being able to be discharged before undergoing further treatment.

The staff at the oncology unit of the Royal Berkshire Hospital under the leadership of Dr Charlton treated and nursed Janet as she underwent a long spell of chemotherapy. On her good weeks we travelled to Spain, and had as good a time as possible.

On 9th June, 2007, we attended the wedding of Gregory and Nicki in St Paul's Cathedral in London, and danced Scottish reels together until late in the evening.

During December 2007, Janet was admitted to The Duchess of Kent Hospice. On 11th December I sat with her and discussed many things as she fell in and out of sleep.

'Jim, I'm not going to be here tomorrow,' she said.

We talked a little longer. She asked for the boys to come

through from the adjoining room, then my sister. Throughout her ordeal that evening, as we left her in a sound sleep, I walked back into her room and she opened her eyes and looked at me. I winked at her. She smiled, closed her eyes and went to sleep.

The following day, 12th December, 2007, we all stood round her bed as she peacefully went into a deeper sleep and left us.

FORTY-SIX
TIME TO FINISH?

Things have changed so much over the years since I joined the Police. The very people who complained about the way they were treated by the police when I was a serving officer took to burning down buildings, rioting and even killing a police officer. Thirty years on, some of these same people are now demanding - as their children are shot and stabbed to death on the streets of Britain - that the police take a firmer hand.

What goes around comes around.

The hands of the Police are tied. Who tied them?

We now have a society where criminality is viewed more as an illness - the cause of which is to be diagnosed in light of our society - rather than as blatant wrongdoing. Politicians, working hand-in-hand with the legal profession, have helped, not to say created, a situation where many criminals receive relatively light sentences in comparison to the severity of their crimes. All the while, the lawyers profit.

Since leaving the police, I have noticed over that period of thirty-five years a steady trend towards politically-correct policing. Moreover, the Force is further bogged down by largely unproductive paperwork and constraining health and safety concerns.

Tommy Wall, the Commandant of the Training School when I joined, would be turning - no, spinning - in his grave, if he were to witness the overall standards in policing today:

A Muslim female officer, in full uniform while on duty, kneeling down to pray on the streets of London.

Buddhist officers refusing to carry truncheons, as they do not believe in using violence.

Dyslexic police officers who are unable to take statements.

Prayer areas being set aside in Police Stations. In 1964, it was discovered that members of the Christian Police Association were praying together before they started work. They were scattered all over the Met area, as it was a disciplinary offence to carry out religious services in a Police Station.

Probationary officers who, after completing and passing their exams at the training college, find it difficult to communicate with the public in English.

What next, blind police officers as dog handlers?

Oh, well, maybe it's me who's become a dinosaur!

In this book I have tried to include as many officers' names as possible that I served with, in what was, and I still believe is, the best police service in the world.

It is coming close to the time to hang up whatever a private investigator hangs up on 'that hook'. I'll find it hard; it has been a pretty busy and rewarding life.

As I approached the end of the writing this book I received a telephone call from a Muslim acquaintance. He asked me to meet with him in central London.

'Jim, here are two names of bad Muslims. I don't want to go to the police with this information.'

He handed me a Post-it note with the two names and their addresses.

'Do what you know best with them.'

I gave the names to a government department. One of the names had been of interest to them, but had gone 'off the radar'. That little bit of paper filled in a crucial space in a very important jigsaw puzzle. Many people will never know how much they owe, perhaps even their lives, to the man with the little Post-it pad.

He doesn't know what the results were of his little note.

Let me say a big thanks to him, on behalf of us all.

Perhaps 'that hook' will stay empty a little longer.

ACKNOWLEDGEMENTS

I would like to thank those who helped me over the years while I was writing the numerous drafts, in particular Jenni Cook.

A number of people wished to remain anonymous. I received a number of indirect enquires from people, who informed me that others were frightened they were going to feature in the book. They can relax, they didn't get a mention - well, not in this one.

My thanks go to the following:

My sister Catherine, Sid and Trish Mackay, Anthony Frewin, Kevin Marwick, Ronnie Morris, Gregory and Nicki, Steven, John and Hillary French, Ross and Phyllis Mackie, Michael Debono and family, Linda and the girls, Les David, Jenny and Gordon Grier, Bernard and Dorothy Tighe, Bob and Cath McInaly, Joelle and family, Dick Kirby.

My gratitude to the staff of the Mijas Hotel, Mijas, Spain for all their kindness over the years, and in particular whilst Janet was undergoing chemotherapy treatment.

INDEX

Note: Ranks are generally the highest mentioned in the text.